Project Portfolio Management

Project Portfolio Management

Leading the corporate vision

Shan Rajegopal, Philip McGuin
and James Waller

First published 2007 by
PALGRAVE MACMILLAN
Houndmills, Basingstoke, Hampshire RG21 6XS and
175 Fifth Avenue, New York, N.Y. 10010
Companies and representatives throughout the world

PALGRAVE MACMILLAN is the global academic imprint of the Palgrave Macmillan division of St. Martin's Press, LLC and of Palgrave Macmillan Ltd. Macmillan® is a registered trademark in the United States, United Kingdom and other countries. Palgrave is a registered trademark in the European Union and other countries.

ISBN-13: 978–0–230–50716–6
ISBN-10: 0–230–50716–6

This book is printed on paper suitable for recycling and made from fully managed and sustained forest sources. Logging, pulping and manufacturing processes are expected to conform to the environmental regulations of the country of origin.

A catalogue record for this book is available from the British Library.

A catalog record for this book is available from the Library of Congress.

10 9 8 7 6 5 4 3 2 1
16 15 14 13 12 11 10 09 08 07

Printed and bound in Great Britain by
Creative Print & Design (Wales), Ebbw Vale

The companies that survive longest are the ones that work out what they uniquely can give to the world – not just growth or money but their excellence, their respect for others, or their ability to make people happy. Some call those things a soul.

Charles Handy

Dedicated
to
All companies seeking excellence in the new economy
May the best you've ever seen be the worst you'll ever see!

CONTENTS

LIST OF FIGURES

FOREWORD

Your organisation has to overcome a variety of challenges in today's business climate and one thing is certain, there will be further obstacles to overcome tomorrow, especially if your business is successful. The challenges and investment in innovation are vital if you are to sustain the longevity of your business. However, I am consistently amazed how much time is spent unnecessarily in meetings and performing mundane tasks that should be second nature in a successful enterprise.

Many organisations employ hundreds or thousands of people who in most cases represent their largest cost. Yet few have visibility of what they are doing or how well they are doing their designated activities, or have no idea of what they are capable of doing.

How many organisations have visibility of their operational costs and deliverables? We read about projects being delayed all the time and of course it always comes as a shock to everyone!

Those who have recognised this and embarked on the implementation of project-centric solutions have often come unstuck due to the complexity of these systems and their inability to obtain compliance throughout their user base. These traditional solutions were conceived from within the engineering industry when they were trying to construct a large building or giant ship. They tended to have a single project focus and concentrated on the timescales associated with achieving the goal rather than the cost of achieving the goal.

Most businesses today have to manage large portfolios of projects, requiring specialist skills from limited skills pools, and are driven by strict project deadlines and budgets. Balancing your workload and your capability is the key to success.

Project Portfolio Management (PPM) has therefore emerged as the next generation of Project Management and is a shift away from one-off, ad hoc approaches to project-centric solutions. PPM establishes a set of values, techniques and technologies that enable visibility, standardisation, measurement and process improvement. PPM enables organisations to manage their projects as a continuous flow of business investments.

Jim Robinson
Head of Programme Delivery
Virgin Mobile

ACKNOWLEDGEMENTS

The outcome of the writing of this book is not due to the sole efforts of the authors as inevitably there are a large number of people who were involved to a greater or lesser extent in the endeavour. The authors have relied on the support, encouragement, enthusiasm and contributions of many. In particular we would like to thank the following, not only for their support but for their continuous encouragement and for giving insightful comments on the book:

Berkshire Consultancy Limited: Mike Robinson, Allen Knight
Atlantic Global Plc: Eugene Blaine, Rupert Hutton, Paul Gleghorn

Berkshire Consultancy extends special thanks to Michael Mobley, a pioneer in project portfolio thinking and who influenced us to achieve a repeatable and scalable process. Other early influencers were William Kern and Peter Heinrich, both of whom have a unique ability to think outside the box and who have encouraged us.

An extra special 'thank you' goes to both Vannesa McGuin and Helen Turner for sharing their thoughts on the various drafts of the manuscript and also for the many hours they dedicated to proofreading.

Dr Shan Rajegopal

Shan is a practitioner, academic and consultant with over 20 years' industrial experience in technology related industries. His career reflects his diverse talents and multidisciplinary interests; however he has a keen interest in the application of Sun Tzu's Art of War as a successful business strategy within the procurement, programmes and change management disciplines. He has held senior positions in culturally diverse organisations in the Far East, USA and Europe, managing, interacting on behalf of and implementing cross-cultural programmes. He was involved in a major technology transfer programme for Hungary under EU funding.

Shan's core skill-sets include programme management implementation and procurement expertise. He has worked with the UK defence industry on assessing, developing and delivering mastery of project management competencies. He has also worked on various blue chip companies' projects within the supply chain covering strategic sourcing, rationalisation of the procurement process, cost improvement and supplier development initiatives. He is also the leading authority on project portfolio management discipline, focusing on bridging the gap between business strategy and effective execution. His comments on this subject have appeared in the *CFO Europe* magazine and *Project Manager Today* magazine.

Shan is a popular speaker at major conferences and seminars worldwide. He has captured his rich experiences in books and contributes articles to journals and magazines. His books include: *Strategic Supply Management: An Implementation Toolkit* and *Sun Tzu and the Project Battleground: Creating Project Strategy from the Art of War*. His work experience covers clients in the aerospace, defence, electronics, finance, IT, minerals and manufacturing sectors.

Philip McGuin

Philip is the E-Business and Product Marketing Manager at Atlantic Global Plc and has been with the company since 2001. He has been responsible for driving the company's e-marketing and product positioning strategy, helping to steer their product offering from an Enterprise

About the authors

Time and Expense application into the professional services and the Project Portfolio Management markets.

Philip has worked within IT for ten years and has specialised in e-business, SaaS and internet product marketing since 1996. He has worked for both the European Parliament and the European Commission, promoting the EU's policy on Information and Communication Technology (ICT), and for the UK Department of Trade and Industry's (DTI) marketing policy on e-government. He has also worked both agency and client side as a senior project consultant on a range of innovative e-business initiatives including e-commerce with Tag Heuer, Powergen, Vernons and BT, online accessibility with the Royal National Institute for the Blind (RNIB) and the Co-operative Bank, and also 'Smile', the UK's first online banking model. At Atlantic Global, Philip is responsible for managing and deploying the company's brand and product range across their e-business platforms and driving the company's competitor and product marketing programme. Prior to his career in the private sector Philip has also worked as a doctoral research fellow on Economic and Monetary Union (EMU) and has lectured in Economics, Politics, and Public Policy and Administration.

James Waller

James was appointed as Head of Marketing at Atlantic Global in June 2004. James has a ten-year track record of building marketing functions and capabilities for growth companies. His previous experience includes time as Director of Corporate Marketing for EMEA at IONA Technologies Plc, an enterprise integration software provider, and prior to that as European Marketing Director at WebGain Inc., an application development tools company. He was also Northern European Marketing Director at IXOS Software AG, a content management software provider. He is responsible for increasing the awareness of Atlantic Global within the emerging marketplace for real-time business software solutions. His role encompasses brand development, marketing communications, direct marketing, investor analysis and press relations.

About Berkshire Consultancy Limited

Berkshire Consultancy Limited is a thriving consultancy practice, providing an integrated range of services to clients in both public and private sectors to meet the challenges of effecting complex organisational change. Berkshire's consultants have the knowledge, skills and experience to work with the tangible or 'hard' aspects of change and improvement, such as business processes, structures, systems and ways of working. They are also skilled in recognising and working with the less tangible or 'soft' aspects represented by organisational cultures and people's values, attitudes and emotional responses. The company believes that most change situations require this holistic approach in order to achieve the best results. In approaching all its projects the company deploys an integrated team to support implementation while embedding culture change to adopt good practices.

The company is sufficiently large to handle a wide range of consultancy assignments and to meet the needs of major organisations. It is small enough to provide a personal, highly tailored and flexible service that is unique to each client. Founded in 1994, the company knows that its business success is directly linked to its ability to provide high quality services to its clients that deliver the results they want, in ways that are constructive and genuinely collaborative. The company cares passionately about adding value and achieving the results its clients need. It is based near Reading, but works across the UK and abroad. Its consultants have worked on a number of international assignments, covering all major continents. It has experience of working with diverse clients from very different organisational and national cultures.

Its consultants are chosen for their business and managerial experience, together with their highly developed interpersonal skills and strong research and academic track records. In addition, each consultant has real expertise in specific areas of business. This mix enables the company to empathise with the opportunities, issues and challenges facing its clients and to offer practical, informed and innovative advice. Its clients say that that they enjoy working with the company, as well as deriving significant value from its consultancy advice and support.

The company's public and private sector clients include the Ministry of Defence, the NHS, the Home Office, the Crown Prosecution Service, NAO, the Cabinet Office, the National Probation Directorate, the Inland Revenue, the UK Passport Office, KPMG, Royal and Sun Alliance, Airbus, MBDA, BAeSystem, Ericsson, Toyota, Hitachi, and UBS among others.

With an international client base spanning the private and public sectors, Berkshire Consultancy Limited provides a fully integrated range of specialist management consultancy services that meet the challenges of effecting organisational change.

Please visit the website at www.berkshire.co.uk.

About Atlantic Global Plc

Atlantic Global Plc is a leading provider of Project Portfolio Management software that enhances the delivery, setup and communication of programmes and projects across the enterprise within both the IT and business operations. It focuses on the discipline of PPM and instils business 'best practice' within the enterprise.

The company delivers an integrated Project Portfolio Management solution that helps organisations who are moving towards a project- and programme-centric way of working. Atlantic Global's flagship product, Corporate Vision, is a powerful Project Portfolio Management software that provides a controlled and predictable method for planning, managing and executing a business's portfolio of projects and programmes as well as enabling it to manage the resource capability of the business more effectively.

Corporate Vision provides a structured environment for deciding which projects, programmes and initiatives to fund, which to sustain and which to kill in order to ensure that they are aligned with corporate strategic objectives. Corporate Vision delivers top-down and bottom-up real-time visibility of key programmes and project information. The Corporate Vision solution seamlessly integrates data from all parts of the business, making it available to everyone who touches the business's projects.

Atlantic Global is currently working with a number of blue chip enterprises (Norwich Union, Barclays, Virgin Mobile, LogicaCMG, GSK, Pfizer, AstraZeneca, Friends Provident, Computacenter, the Metropolitan Police, Provident Financial, HSBC, Serco, ManGroup Plc, Orange, Xchanging, Hemsley Fraser, Harvey Nash, and Crown Agents) as well as local and central government.

Please visit the website at www.atlantic-global.com.

Who should read the book

This book is for executives and business leaders who need to manage projects as business investments and to measure their impact on the bottom line. It is also for programme, project, and resource portfolio managers who need to improve their methods of managing multi-project environments and to ensure that they are able to make their projects accountable to the corporate goals of the business.

Benefits of the book

Project Portfolio Management (PPM) is about ensuring you have the correct mix of projects that are focused on taking the business where it has decided to go. It is about being able to respond quickly to changes in the environment, enabling the business to set the direction and then create a series of steps to get there.

This book is a practical business guide to implementing PPM and is designed to help you:

- understand what Project Portfolio Management is about and why it is important
- build an effective process for your company using best practice processes and software tools to support PPM deployment
- kick-start the process in a realistic and workable environment, which is 'low risk' to the business yet 'high value' in its potential return on investment.
- execute and implement the process of PPM
- embed a sustainable PPM model within the business environment
- execute a PPM process that enables the business to manage the detailed projects process itself as well as delivering the portfolio perspective required to inform the business of their impact, with specific reference to the following:
  - measuring performance to ensure that projects are collectively meeting the portfolio strategy
  - identifying, qualifying, and funding projects that address the business strategy

- o enforcing a collaborative effort that enables senior executives to reach agreement on project portfolio objectives
- o better managing organisational resource demand, capacity, and capability
- o understanding how much your projects are costing the business
- o aligning your projects with the business's strategic goals
- o managing multiple projects/programmes via the Programme Management Office (PMO)
- o giving key project and portfolio stakeholder role based visibility
- o understanding better how to resolve resource conflicts between projects
- o maintaining visibility of key project information across the enterprise
- o acquiring the benefits of real-time reporting in order to drive portfolio decision making
- o evaluating your organisation's current readiness for PPM
- o understanding your organisation's current strengths, weaknesses and gaps within the project management process

Structure of the book

The structure of the book is depicted in a simple step-by-step guide to the chapters, as shown in Figure 1. This approach is also very process

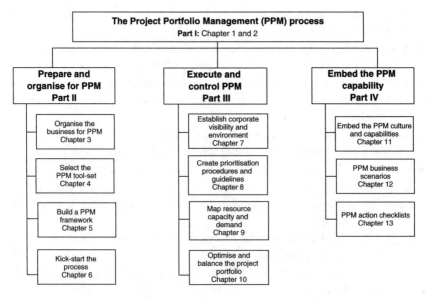

Figure 1 Structure of the book

oriented and as a result can be used by an organisation as a way of deploying PPM.

Part I Understand Project Portfolio Management

The first part of the book explores the origins of PPM and discusses the many demands placed upon project oriented businesses today. We then go on to define PPM, and discuss its relationship with programme and project management. Finally we discuss why PPM is important to the business and some of the adoption challenges facing organisations when deploying PPM.

Part II Prepare and organise for Project Portfolio Management

This part examines what the business needs to do to organise the people, processes and tools.

People

We explore issues behind organising executive sponsorship, the Project Portfolio Management Team (PPMT), the Programme Management Office (PMO) and rolling out role based visibility for executive, portfolio, programme, project, and resource managers as well as team members.

Tools

We examine the necessary software features and capabilities needed when implementing a PPM software solution. We also discuss many of the software implementation dos and don'ts and we provide a best practice checklist and software roadmap.

Process

We then turn to the processes/methodologies that need to be considered for the project portfolio framework. These include the definition, selection, prioritisation and pipeline processes. Finally we look at how the business can kick-start the PPM process by deploying a 'low risk', 'high value' proof-of-benefit (PoB) model. The PoB de-risks the process of organising and deploying a PPM solution, allowing the business to deal with 'chunks' of activity that prove the value of the solution and processes from one stage to the next.

Part III Execute and control Project Portfolio Management

This part depicts a step-by-step guide to how a PPM process can be implemented. A key emphasis in this part of the book is that the execution of PPM must be managed as a business transformation project.

Part IV Embed the Project Portfolio Management capability

This final part of the book argues that the greatest challenge in PPM implementation is embedding and sustaining the PPM capability within an organisation. It shows the cultural resistance that can occur as a result of business process change and it argues that a PPM deployment must follow a sound change management plan. It further argues that to sustain PPM capability the Project Portfolio Management Team needs to develop a knowledge management strategy as part of the change management plan. It finally discusses the benefits of realisation management as a way to embed a PPM capability culture.

THE TEN COMMANDMENTS OF PPM

There are a variety of fundamental factors that are absolutely essential to the successful implementation of a PPM process and solution. We have called these factors 'The Ten Commandments of PPM' and they form the foundation of this book.

These Ten Commandments are:

1. **View projects as business investments**: Project Portfolio Management is not just another project management process – it is about how the business manages projects as strategic short, medium and long term investments. PPM looks to empower the business, not just the project process. From the strategic viewpoint it allows stakeholders, business leaders and executives to see clearly and understand how effective their strategies are and if necessary which programmes and projects to review. From the operational viewpoint PPM empowers the portfolio, programme, resource and project managers with the tools, support and necessary corporate accountability to execute project delivery.

2. **Achieve the correct balance between processes, people and tools**: Implementing PPM involves a careful blend of people, processes and tools. Success is based on the balancing of all three and ensuring the correct tool selection, for example, ensuring that software is designed to support, aid and improve process effectiveness and efficiency. Remember, do not let software bend and break your business's backbone, nor allow processes to bog down and adversely affect your organisation culture.

3. **Aim for low risk, high value deployment**: Avoid a 'big bang' or 'rip-and-replace' approach and look to deploy PPM in bite-size chunks, by developing a proof of benefit or 'model office'. This approach provides an actual, real-world view of the value of a PPM solution within a low risk environment and is an excellent way to communicate its potential return on investment (ROI) and return on opportunity (ROO).

4. **Ensure business-wide visibility**: Enterprise- or business-wide visibility is delivered through the deployment of role based dashboards. Role based dashboards are designed to empower all project stakeholders within the business with project information that is relevant to their role and position. Role based visibility is about providing fast and effective means of integrating the strategic with the operational

and delivering a practical means for real-time opportunity detection. Role based visibility enables the business to drill through layers of management and is designed to provide business and project leaders with the ability to spot project redundancies, resource appropriately, understand budget allocation and spend, as well as keeping close tabs on project progress and how it impacts on the bottom line.

5. **Establish a single version of the truth**: Implement a process that accesses project information from a single data source in a real-time environment. A single point of entry keeps information consistent, accurate, complete and also ensures that the management has a single, reliable version of the truth. This single data source removes delays to management and execution of critical business processes.

6. **Negotiate executive sponsorship**: Sponsorship from the top provides an infrastructure whereby the right authority is empowered to drive the right behaviour in the organisation and ensures that the deployment of PPM is strategically driven. In others words, a truly strategy driven approach to managing an organisation's projects must start at the top in order for accountability and transparency to extend throughout the organisation and to lend the PPM process both credibility and suitability.

7. **Implement as a change project**: The implementation of Project Portfolio Management has to be managed not only as a project but as a change management project. Introducing the Project Portfolio Management process is a business process change initiative and as a result the leadership involvement and cultural change expected from the stakeholders are fundamental for the successful implementation of the portfolio process. A process champion must be actively engaged in using, funding, promoting, and defending Project Portfolio Management. Senior managers, functional managers, and project managers must understand the portfolio management objectives and processes. They must be actively involved in pushing the approved processes out to the organisation and be willing to enforce the process and deliverable requirements.

8. **Develop project management competence and maturity**: Project managers must have the skills and tools available to them to produce quality project plans. A quality project plan indicates there is a high degree of confidence in the project manager's ability to identify the tasks necessary to meet the project objectives and to provide good estimates for the resources required to accomplish the tasks.

9. **Define an agreed and accepted PPM process**: The PPM process defined and established must be a consistent and repeatable process that captures project and portfolio metrics that enable consistent

comparison over time across projects and the portfolio. It must be a process that obliges organisational staff to work together as a team and share resources across departments, thereby improving resource utilisation and increasing the return on investment from the portfolio of projects accomplished.

10. **Embed PPM capability in everyday business working**: The Project Portfolio Management outputs (reports, and so on) must be used to guide decision making and enforce the process. When staff see managers are using this data to make decisions, they will want to keep their own project elements accurate and up to date. Furthermore, it is important to provide PPM process oversight and support to ensure staff are properly educated to contribute to the portfolio management process.

PART I

Understand Project Portfolio Management

Within this opening part of the book we will explore some of the key issues that have influenced the processes of enterprise planning and project management in recent years and the effect that these have had on elevating PPM onto the radar of many business and executive agendas today:

- Firstly, we explore the demands of project management within a complex enterprise environment. We examine why projects have become a core facet of the way businesses are run today and why organisations are ensuring that project processes are subjected to a higher level of strategic rigour and accountability.
- Secondly, we discuss the impact of IT portfolio management on the emergence of Project Portfolio Management and show why businesses are using their experiences here to bring greater project discipline into the wider business framework.
- Thirdly, we look at the common misconceptions about Project Portfolio Management, and how it differs from traditional approaches to managing projects within the business. We then look at defining Project Portfolio Management and understanding why it is important for business today.
- Finally, we turn to the practical consideration of determining the common problems that businesses face when managing projects and how Project Portfolio Management seeks to address these issues. We also look at best practice PPM implementation considerations and some of the adoption and change management challenges facing businesses.

CHAPTER 1

Defining Project Portfolio Management

1.1 Enterprise project management

Competition, new product development, mergers, outsourcing and off-shoring all result in change and in today's business climate 'change' is the only constant. As enterprises are forced to adapt dynamically to changing market conditions this necessitates engaging in the management of multi-project environments.

As projects represent a significant investment for the organisation, attention is focused on the value of those projects to the business. Projects are no longer 'one-off' isolated distractions, but a core facet of the business, increasingly subjected to a high level of rigour and accountability.

A project in a business environment may encompass initiatives of a diverse nature such as enterprise-wide IT, business transformation, construction and the implementation of regulatory compliance measures. Whatever the initiative, projects are an integral part of the business and are a key vehicle for realising business strategy.

Executives have come to realise that projects form the future profitability and ultimately the success of their organisations. Therefore there is a growing interest on the part of business leaders in how their projects are performing and impacting the bottom line. When it comes to measuring the success of the business's projects it was once said that executives focused just on two things: (1) when they will be finished and (2) what they will cost. However, today executives focus instead on managing the right mix of long, medium and short term projects, understanding which projects will provide the best utilisation of resources, maximise the ROI benefit for the busines's, and deliver against corporate strategic objectives and to specification.

With stakeholders demanding greater accountability, executives are faced with the increased complexity of managing multidimensional project environments across many levels and facets of the organisation. For executives to drive project success they need access to consistent and comparable information about all projects in their organisation. But project information is often scattered across different departments and business units, making it difficult to execute informed decisions about where to invest scarce resources, how to prioritise initiatives and balance project demands. Generally speaking, many enterprises manage their projects poorly and under some circumstances, management works hard to keep project problems out of sight and out of mind.

KPMG conducted a recent survey that strongly suggested that project performance in many businesses is still sub-standard. In other words, organisations do not appear to be delivering on their commitments. These commitments are being sacrificed, the required value from project investments is not being achieved and consequently the discipline of project management is coming under scrutiny.

Not only do many organisations lack a tactical infrastructure but they also lack strategic visibility over project activity. From the tactical view-point many businesses possess no consistent method of project planning, no real-time view of resource capability and little or no method of reporting project health and status. Nor do they have the ability accurately to roll up this data to the executive team in real time and on demand. From the strategic view-point many businesses lack a dynamic process for understanding project benefit realisation, value and prioritising as well as empowering the executive team with the ability to make 'buy, sell or hold' decisions in order to balance projects as business investments. Consequently, project selections are frequently based on subjective factors such as political influences or perceived, rather than actual, value.

Many organisations suffer from project failures and programme inefficiencies as a result of inadequate sponsorship from the top, poor governance and compliance, poor project prioritisation and/or projects conflicting with day-to-day operations. As well as scope creep, lack of project accountability and poor definition of expectations, project problems are also exacerbated by the absence of a formal framework for tying and managing projects within the context of the business's vision and goals.

Moreover, KPMG also argue that complexity, organisational change impact, duration and size influence the rate of project failure.

Even those companies that have attempted to deploy a project, programme or portfolio system have too often been given bad advice and have poured huge sums of money into systems that promise 'project utopia'. The reasons for this are numerous yet one consistent problem that traditionally plagues the business community is that they have been subjected to a plethora of software vendors and consultancies who build their solution from the bottom up using pure project-centric tools and methods with little vision of how this will tie into the business. There is a 'graveyard' of nightmare stories in which organisations waste millions of pounds on cumbersome systems that were destined never to work, simply because they did not address the issue of what the business actually needed. Both large and small corporations have found themselves shoe-horning solutions and process with a message from vendors that typically says, *'There's nothing wrong with our method; it's the shape of your business that's wrong.'* The results is that all too often, these systems leave the companies worse off – financially, operationally and with the inability to plan and implement their business's projects effectively.

Whether your business is 'small or large', project environments are multidimensional: they have sub-projects or child projects involving multiple timeframes, multiple departments, multiple suppliers and multiple locations, touching every part of the business. However, the most valuable asset and the greatest liability lie in the people, tools and processes used to manage the projects. Businesses are continually confronted with the challenge of tying together disparate processes and locations, multiple disciplines, technologies and departments as well as managing non-finite resources and budgets. Businesses no longer manage their projects as static or isolated linear entities but as complex interdependencies. The factors driving project management within an enterprise environment involve the multifaceted collaborations of the business's ability to successfully execute the key project components seamlessly and as a natural extension of the business rather than as separate, alien entities. These typically include:

- managing the supply of non-finite resources, roles and responsibilities both internal and external to the business
- communicating project information such as budgets, milestones and resource capability through layers of management and across multiple physical locations
- managing and controlling the flow of project documentation ranging from contractor quotes to risk mitigation, project charters and so on
- developing multiple processes that bring project information to those occupying the relevant roles and responsibilities
- building business cases, outlining project objectives and specifying project scope
- establishing criteria for assessing ROI and measuring the compliance of the completed project with its original objectives
- communicating strategic objectives to all stakeholders with an interest in the project

- defining the relationships between all internal and external resource groups
- managing the flow of information between all project stakeholders
- managing project approval and direction at each appropriate level within the business
- agreeing specifications, milestones and governance criteria for project deliverables
- outlining the assignment of project roles and responsibilities at both the strategic and operational levels
- publishing project plans that span all project stages from project initiation and development through to delivery
- adopting a process of distilling upstream and downstream project status and progress reporting
- implementing a best practice knowledge-base centre such as a Programme Management Office (PMO)
- addressing risk management and resolution of issues that arise during the project
- defining a standard for quality review of the key governance documents and of the project deliverables

1.2 IT portfolio management

Even though Project Portfolio Management builds upon the Project Management and Professional Services Automation techniques of the 1980s and 1990s, it has its origin within corporate IT and the management of Information Technology projects. What is more commonly termed *IT portfolio management* emerged at the end of the so called 'dot.com boom' in 2000 as a consequence of many failed IT projects, and borrows extensively from the financial community as a method of balancing investment risk and opportunity.

Over the last ten years IT has become an integral part of the business and is fundamental to the future growth and profitability of most large IT based organisations today. However, the seemingly unreachable goals of IT and business alignment have dominated the boardroom top ten lists for over a decade. Indeed, the ability of the enterprise to effectively bridge the gap between corporate business objectives and the associated demands and constraints of technology execution have been suspect at best.

A key, characteristic theme of IT portfolio management is that IT projects can no longer function within an inaccessible 'black box'. Nor can IT be the sole domain of IT departments who ring-fence technical intellectual property, skills and knowledge.

The ongoing need for alignment between IT and the business has become the critical driving force behind the adoption of portfolio management techniques within recent years. For example, IT analysts Gartner have conducted extensive research into IT portfolio management and have identified the following key drivers that concern CIOs:

- delivering IT projects that enable business growth
- linking business and IT strategy and plans
- demonstrating the business value of IT
- applying metrics to IT organisation and services
- improving IT governance
- developing leadership in the senior IT team
- improving business opportunity readiness

There still remains widespread problematic handling of IT projects by board-level executives as well as senior management and this has largely been due to:

- limited technical knowledge and experience
- project complexity and scope
- changing pace of the IT market
- key decisions being deferred mainly to pure technical experts
- inability of the organisation to tie its projects into the business and make them accountable

Businesses therefore tackle IT planning at the project level and make decisions about system upgrades and software implementation with little or no analysis performed to understand their impact on the organisation's overall direction and goals.

1.2.1 How have IT portfolio management techniques sought to overcome these problems and how has their adoption impacted the wider business?

IT portfolio management borrows directly from the financial planning and investment community. This community uses a series of portfolio investment techniques that focus on goals, risk levels, costs, and forecasted returns, as the principle roadmap for investment. If for example the set of goals within a financial portfolio are growth, income and capital preservation, decision making is concerned with how much of the portfolio should be dedicated to each category. Tactical decisions are then used to support this decision making by determining which investments to sell, retain or buy within the various portfolio categories. What is critical here is that decisions are made on the basis of the entire context of the portfolio. This stands in stark contrast to IT planning which traditionally takes a bottom-up, rather than top-down perspective, with little or no consideration given to how individual project decisions affect the business as a whole. The financial planning method has been adopted as a means of planning IT projects and has migrated within recent years into the wider domain as a method by which the business as a whole can plan.

IT portfolio management emphasises a strategic focus on goals such as revenue growth, cost reduction, regulatory mandate and business continuity rather than just typical operational objectives such as project cost, timescales and deliverables. IT portfolio management requires input from across the organisation, including finance managers, executive management, and business groups, as well as IT managers. With IT portfolio management, project planning is viewed as a fundamentally top-down initiative and all project based stakeholders, including the board, internal and external stakeholders are required to participate in the decision making process. IT portfolio management moves away from the project-centric, bottom-up approach, forces everyone to accept responsibility for critical systems, and is designed to prevent a single stakeholder, for example IT, being blamed for poor decisions. The key driver behind IT portfolio management is gaining visibility of all of the business demands being placed on IT and elevating performance through the effective use of resources, people, funding, assets and processes – in order to maximise business value.

The typical core components of IT portfolio management are outlined below. We will see later that these elements also form the basis of Project Portfolio Management and we will explain in detail how these key elements form the basis of your PPM framework.

- *Building a registry*: Portfolio management begins with gathering a detailed registry of all the projects in the company, ideally in a single database, including name, length, estimated cost, business objective, ROI and business benefits.
- *Identifying strategic objectives*: This involves the business compiling a list of projects during the annual planning cycle and supporting them with business cases that show estimated costs, ROI, business benefit and risk assessment and so on. One of the core criteria on which projects get funded is how closely a project meets the company's strategic objectives for the upcoming year.
- *Prioritising and categorising*: The prioritisation process allows the business to fund the projects that most closely align with your

company's strategic objectives. The business then attaches valuation criteria to rank projects in terms of their importance.

- *Managing and reviewing the portfolio*: The portfolio has to be actively managed and monitored. Many businesses use a centralised Programme Management Office (PMO) to get financial and work progress perspective updates from project leaders. This information goes into a database and is reported to executives via a Project Portfolio Management Team (PPMT), giving the project inventory and its status. Typically businesses use the RAG method – Red (help!), Amber (caution) or Green (good) – to identify project status and this includes an explanation of the key driver causing an Amber or Red condition. Usually a portfolio team convenes to make decisions to continue or stop initiatives, assess funding levels and resolve resource issues.

IT portfolio management has revolutionised how businesses manage their projects and has delivered the following benefits:

- better cooperation across IT, finance, executive management and operational departments
- unified application for all planning, resource management, forecasting, and reporting, which provides a single, accurate version of the facts
- tighter alignment with organisational objectives; initiatives are scored on their support for strategic objectives in order to demonstrate their value to the business
- maximised portfolio value with optimal balance, enabling the business to select, win, and retain desirable projects while maintaining a balanced portfolio based on acceptable risk, changing business objectives and varied investment types
- increased transparency and better decision making; information is unified, enabling stakeholders to identify underperforming or overlapping projects, risks, and resource bottlenecks sooner and make midcourse adjustments
- better resource utilisation; demand for resources is captured, prioritised, and matched to the available supply
- improved portfolio governance; an automated, role based workflow streamlines and enforces approval for funding, resource assignments, gate decisions, and ongoing evaluations
- delivery of real-time data for effective decision making and performance transparency
- creation of a single database that shows the immediate impact of changes to the numbers in real time

The IT portfolio management processes have been directly translated into the wider business environment and their component parts have formed the basis of PPM as a methodology for managing projects within the wider context of the business. Albeit portfolio management techniques are firmly rooted within IT, they no longer have sole ownership. Portfolio principles are now being used to add value across an enterprise and over the last several years PPM has been adapted to measure the performance of many businesses' collective set of projects across all major areas including finance, R&D, new product development, sales, marketing and so on.

PPM is still relatively immature with both vendors and consultancies still jostling for market position, while its adoption among businesses is still very much in its infancy. However, over the next few years PPM will become a standard instrument and process for project focused organisations. Drivers to its adoption include governance demands, organisational change, business transformation, off-shoring, outsourcing and maturity through initiatives such as CMMI and Six Sigma.

1.3   The Project Portfolio Management paradigm

PPM is a paradigm shift in thinking, its successful implementation driven from the top down, spearheaded by executive and senior management sponsorship and responsibility. PPM attempts to straddle the gap between the projects themselves, the management process and their accountability to the business. PPM is the bridging that brings together the strategic and the operational.

PPM challenges the narrow 'pure play, project-by-project orientated focus to planning' and draws attention to the broader, more integrated approach, which subjects projects to wider organisational considerations and executive responsibility.

Simply put, PPM looks to empower the business, not just the project process. It helps the business establish a clear line of sight from the top-level pan-initiative view right down to the individual project layer. From the strategic viewpoint, it allows stakeholders, business leaders and executives to see clearly and understand how effective their strategies are and if necessary which programmes and projects to review. From the operational viewpoint, PPM empowers programme, resource and project managers with tools, support and necessary corporate accountability to execute project delivery.

1.4   What is Project Portfolio Management?

Driving project performance is not only about 'doing projects right'; it is about 'doing the right projects'. Yet doing the right projects is about more than simply individual project selection, rather it is about how the organisation manages the entire mix of the business's portfolio of projects. It is about achieving a level of visibility over project delivery that enables the business to make calculated 'go/kill/hold/fix' decisions and ensure rational, accurate alignment with the business. It is ultimately about how the business sees projects as investments within the short, medium and long term. PPM can therefore be defined as:

> The management of the project portfolio so as to maximise the contribution of projects to the overall welfare and success of the enterprise. Project Portfolio Management (PPM) is the management of that collection of projects and programmes in which a company invests to implement its strategy, for example asset programmes, improvement initiatives and strategic change work streams among others. A PPM process can utilise various techniques to provide tangible results for your business, ensuring that project investments contribute directly to realising your corporate goals.

It is simply not enough for the business to manage the project mix without the management of the projects themselves. When organising the business for PPM it is important to understand that there is a fine balance between the actual detailed management of the projects themselves and the portfolio perspective required to inform the business of their impact. In other words:

- Project Portfolio Management is critical for decision making, governance, and to ensure your company's business objectives are being supported by the right set of projects.
- Project management is critical to ensure that budgets, resource allocation, activity and work are accurate and delivered on time.

Both are required to ensure the right set of projects are selected and that they are delivered on time, within budget and scope.

Therefore let's expand our definition of PPM by saying that it also refers to:

> The organisation of a series of projects into a portfolio consisting of reports that capture project objectives, costs, timelines, accomplishments, resources, risks and other critical factors. PPM enables regular review of entire portfolios, allocation of resources and adjustment of projects to assist in taking key financial and business decisions in order produce the highest returns. In addition, PPM helps bridge the strategic and operational by enable the business's 'coal face' to deliver on the project management process.

PPM is not only about how the modern, project oriented business manages its projects as strategic business investments but also about how it actually manages the project process itself and how this iterative process is communicated back and forth throughout the business.

1.5 The relationship between portfolios, programmes and projects

A project portfolio represents the collection of programmes and projects (see Figure 2); as outlined above, the process of PPM includes oversight, management and control of these components.

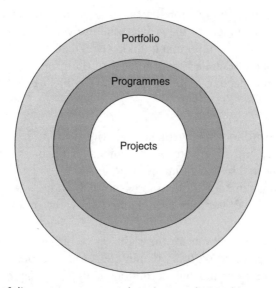

Figure 2 Portfolio, programmes and projects: relationships

Project Portfolio Management provides a structured environment for deciding which projects, programmes and initiatives to fund, to sustain or to eliminate. Project Portfolio Management is the process that enables the right programmes and project to be selected and takes into account the business's capability to deliver on these projects set against the available financial and human resources. It is also about optimising the overall portfolio investment, and subordinating programme and project approval to business strategy rather than departmental and business unit objectives.

1.5.1 Defining portfolios

Figure 3 shows that the Project Portfolio Management process serves as a continuous mechanism to ensure that projects remain aligned with their strategic intent, that assumptions defined in their original business case

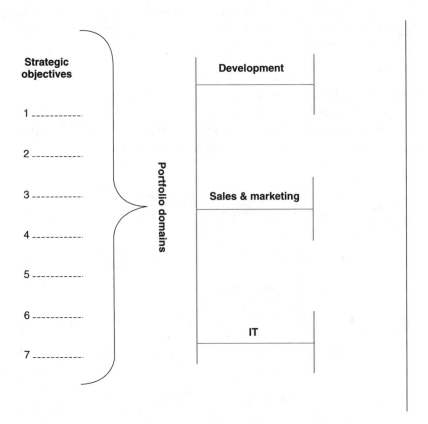

Figure 3 Strategic objectives and project portfolio domains

are adhered to and that decisions made during development are based on timely and accurate data. By their very nature, timelines, budgets, scope and project teams change over time. The PPM process therefore seeks to provide real-time data that can assist in making daily project decisions, as well as more analytical 'what if' scenarios that can direct the future course of the individual portfolio domains.

1.5.2   Defining programmes

As can be seen from Figure 4, programme management is the process of managing multiple, ongoing, interdependent projects. Programme management is comprised both of operational initiatives that enable real-isation of business value, and of groupings of activities and projects that enable the implementation of a strategy and seek its outcome. The figure shows the strategic alignment of projects, programmes and project portfolio for delivery optimisation. Programmes are more fluid and are directed at a goal or set of objectives, rather than specific deliverables; they are focused on outcomes rather than outputs; and they are about business management as well as technical management.

1.5.3   Defining projects

Projects are a series of planned activities with clearly defined start and end points and clearly defined deliverables. Projects manage the estimated

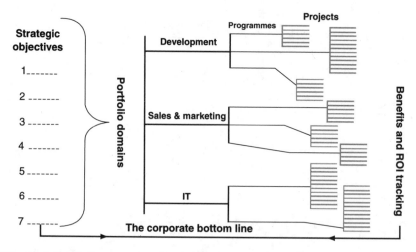

Figure 4 Portfolio, programme and project portfolio domains

Project life cycle

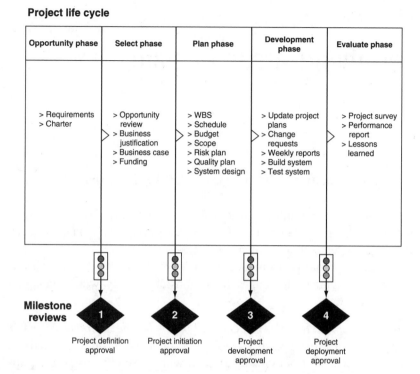

Opportunity phase	Select phase	Plan phase	Development phase	Evaluate phase
> Requirements > Charter	> Opportunity review > Business justification > Business case > Funding	> WBS > Schedule > Budget > Scope > Risk plan > Quality plan > System design	> Update project plans > Change requests > Weekly reports > Build system > Test system	> Project survey > Performance report > Lessons learned

Milestone reviews

1	2	3	4
Project definition approval	Project initiation approval	Project development approval	Project deployment approval

Figure 5 Typical project life cycle and stage gate process

and actual start and completion dates for project tasks and these tasks are the building blocks for project delivery. Projects are usually managed as part of a life cycle, in a sequence of phases (or steps) from project initiation through to project completion (see Figure 5). Typically the project life cycle follows this sequence: opportunity, selection, planning, development, evaluation. There are approval points or gates between each phase. Typical gates include:

1 definition approval
2 initiation approval
3 development approval
4 deployment approval

CHAPTER 2

Identifying areas of pain

2.1 Typical project challenges faced by businesses

One of the most common issues facing companies today is that they concentrate their management efforts on executing individual projects, but fail to understand the impact of these on the wider business. The result is sub-optimal performance and lower returns for the business as a whole. The typical challenges facing business today when managing projects include:

- *Misalignment between projects and their business objectives*: The purpose of a project is to advance one or more business objectives. Most projects start out closely aligned with these objectives, but gaps inevitably appear. Projects drift and business objectives change and evolve. Without redirection, projects and deliverables end up failing to meet expectations.
- *Late or delayed projects*: Late projects wreak havoc, delaying the time at which a company can start reaping business benefits, thwarting precise payback period calculations and disrupting the long term return on investment.
- *Dependency conflicts*: Most projects are interrelated, sharing people, equipment, resources and deliverables. These dependencies mean that a single project delay has a significant ripple effect on related projects, disrupting schedules, causing resource conflicts and even triggering expensive contingencies, in order to minimise risks.
- *Execution difficulties*: Problematic execution wastes resources, time and opportunities, diverts management attention and hinders project delivery.
- *Overlapping and redundant projects*: Overlapping projects are responsible for major inefficiencies and wasted budgets, time and resources. At their worst, they undermine each other's progress and potential benefits. Redundant and duplicative projects are also unprofitable, increasing costs, prolonging schedules and diverting resources from more deserving projects.

- *Resource conflicts*: Companies rarely have sufficient resources to staff all projects concurrently. As such, projects compete against each other for resources, and people are often assigned to several projects at the same time. Those with special expertise or scarce skills may be in high demand, causing bottlenecks.
- *Unrealised business value*: A project is a means to an end. Ultimately, every project generates deliverables that the company uses to derive business value. When those deliverables arrive late or are incomplete, the business loses opportunities – whether to earn revenues, acquire customers or perhaps fix a problem.
- *Diffuse decision making*: Many executives are unable to obtain the right information at the right time to effectively understand the present position of the business in order to communicate unwelcome surprises and/or communicate potential opportunities before the competition.
- *No accountability*: Failure to continuously monitor and communicate project milestones in real time, and budget performance, dilutes project accountability and responsibility.
- *Fragmentation*: Fragmented planning and resource processes and tools lead to an inability to systematically communicate and fine-tune multiple project scenarios, resulting in regular unforeseen slippage and problems.

Before we can plan for PPM, areas of pain need to be identified. Below is a basic checklist of all typical pain areas:

- failure to link project delivery with business growth
- lack of strategic alignment and of clear goals and objectives
- no real-time visibility of project status and activity
- objectives changing during the project
- unrealistic time or resource estimates
- lack of executive support and user involvement
- failure to communicate and act as a team
- poor planning, accountability and communication
- poor resource allocation and inappropriate skills
- disparate technical systems
- lack of senior business sponsorship
- poor or undefined communication of project objectives
- lack of communication between the project management shop floor and the business
- poor communication of project and resource information across the enterprise

- no governance contract – that is, unreliable two-way commitment between the business and operations on why, how and when projects are delivered
- management unable to access, in real time, reports on projects and operations to measure progress and make decisions
- poor data quality and consistency as a result of using semi-manual software applications such as spreadsheets
- revenue leakage and poor auditing of financial and project transactions due to slow, inconsistent and sometimes inaccurate data
- inability to roll up project/programme status and milestones in real time through layers of management
- greater administrative overhead as a result of using semi-manual software applications such as spreadsheets to track and manage projects
- inability to anticipate projects going over budget and/or out of scope before the event
- inability to integrate project data such as timesheets and expenses into payroll and accounting systems
- inability to forecast resource gaps or resource overload and to balance out model resource utilisation scenarios
- poor capacity planning and scheduling, leading to increased bench time for key resources
- poor tracking of staff skills and availability, leading to inability to forecast resource requirements and analyse impact of new projects
- lack of standardised planning and project management procedures and practices

2.2   Why implement Project Portfolio Management?

Is there a business today, no matter how large or small, that can afford to invest in non-performing or non-strategic projects? The importance of investing in the right projects, the need for compliance and the urgent demand for new product and service development all provide reasons why businesses depend on their project management processes to deliver and optimise results.

It is a fact that businesses operate in a complex environment with many programmes and projects going on at any one time. Project Portfolio Management is today seen as an essential prerequisite not only for driving and improving project performance, but also for ensuring the business's success. The reality is that in all organisations decision making is not an easy task for the executive team. Making 'effective' and 'efficient' decisions about a project, based on rational, accurate and real-time data, can be virtually impossible. For example – projects are often arbitrarily assessed only against the bottom-line financial impact instead of being evaluated according to their health, cost and strategic contribution to the organisation over the short and long term.

Essentially many businesses lack the day-to-day tools and processes needed to facilitate the discussion and resolution of difficult project decisions. They lack the standardised processes which help project stakeholders throughout the organisation understand how and why certain decisions are being made and also enable the business to ferret out so-called 'pet projects' that do not contribute to strategic objectives. Even when organisations embark upon developing a formal framework for aligning their projects with the business process it is still fraught with roadblocks (see section 2.3). Many organisations are still daunted by the perceived capital and cultural investment needed to deploy PPM, and many organisations still ask whether they need such a process to manage their business projects and whether the cultural and technical impact is palatable. Figure 6 highlights the potential cost of not deploying PPM and the impact that this may have on the business.

PPM enables the business to align resources and project investments with corporate objectives. PPM provides a structured environment for deciding which projects, programmes and initiatives to fund, to sustain and to eliminate. PPM is about optimising the investment in change initiatives and subordinating programme and project approval to business strategy rather than departmental and business unit objectives. PPM ensures you are running the right programmes and brings discipline to the project muddle and resource contention that are so common in large

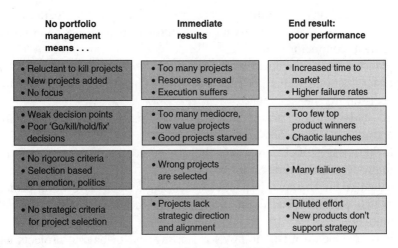

Figure 6 Consequences of not implementing PPM

organisations. PPM is the management of a portfolio so as to maximise the contribution of projects to the overall welfare and success of the enterprise.

For business leaders and executives this means that:

- Projects should contribute to a positive cash flow for the enterprise.
- Projects must effectively utilise the organisation's resources.
- Projects must help position the organisation for future success and growth.

The PPM process enables business users to organise a series of projects into an integrated portfolio. As part of this process the business is able to produce reports based on the various project objectives, costs, resources and risks. This will assist the business in making key financial and business decisions. PPM is a dynamic process whereby projects are regularly evaluated, prioritised and selected, based on the goal of obtaining the greatest possible value from the organisation's limited resources.

PPM enables the organisation to:

- meet financial and business governance milestone costs effectively
- bring new products to market in line with business strategy only when resource capability and budget restrictions allow
- implement outsourcing and off-shoring initiatives with real-time visibility of operational time, cost and resource information across business units
- track and optimise lights-on activity to aid business growth and efficiency drives
- understand resource utilisation and profitability, allowing better alignment of resources, more dynamic workforce management and reductions in contractor costs
- reduce reporting timescales at executive and board level, allowing faster reactions to market and competitive changes and more accurate decision making
- get early warning of any potential problems in meeting programme and project milestones
- make it easy for different stakeholders to access project information relevant to their strategic interests
- calculate the financial impact of cancelling a poor-performing project
- switch priorities based on organisational needs and redeploy staff quickly
- have a standard methodology for starting and managing projects and making them accountable to the business

- reduce programme and project overruns and costs
- reduce programme and project duplication and effort
- track costs, revenues and margins for each project in the portfolio
- learn from past projects
- account for cost of time spent on projects
- reduce the risk of losing money on projects
- identify risks at the outset and their impact on the business
- understand how changes to one project will affect other projects
- identify projects that are not contributing to objectives
- reduce the risk of skills shortages at critical times
- track delivery against key milestones

2.3 Change management and adoption challenges

The implementation of PPM brings more openness to the authorisation process and less ambiguity into the what, where, when and how of the project delivery process. If a PPM process is put in place typical political manipulation around pet projects becomes much more difficult. PPM also makes it difficult to hide mistakes and brings a level of detail that may create a fear factor amongst both senior and operational managers. However PPM is a change project and resistance to change will essentially become the norm.

There's no single right way to deploy PPM; software vendors, consulting companies and academics all offer a variety of models and techniques. But there are plenty of hurdles to doing it well and ensuring that the business is able to deploy a sustainable implementation with credibility and longevity. In Parts II and III of this book we will explore in more detail how to organise the business for PPM, the change management steps necessary for a successful deployment, and how to embed it within the business. However, before we explore these issues in detail, here are the barriers to adoption and some of the key challenges confronting the business:

- Internal politics and culture are by far the biggest barriers to adoption. PPM by its very nature will demand change within the business, and with change comes resistance – from both above and below.
- You will need to become an 'evangelist' for Project Portfolio Management, with an 'executive sponsored guardian angel'. Resistance is inevitable; critics will most likely outnumber advocates, and you will need to continually preach the benefits and prove the value of PPM.

- Often management is aware of dissenters or non-conformists in the organisation, but mistakenly relies upon the introduction of the new system to improve these individuals' productivity and performance, rather than tackling them head-on through direct communication before introducing the new system.
- Organisational capability and maturity in programme and project management governance and standards will impact PPM adoption. The more mature the organisation's project management capability, the more ready will the business be to adopt PPM.
- Top management commitment to and understanding of the purpose and value of Project Portfolio Management is critical. Typically senior management either delegates it to lower ranks, or believes that it is the responsibility of the vendor to design and implement a complete process in isolation, and fails to appreciate that the organisation and its key personnel are a vital part of the adoption process.
- Inability of management to agree criteria for identifying projects within the organisation is an important barrier. For example, there will be resistance from programme and project teams to the adoption of a common approach to managing projects, reporting progress and constructing business cases.
- Unwillingness of business managers to see their pet projects shifted in priority is also a barrier.
- Disagreement on the pace of adoption is a challenge. Whether rollout is incremental or rapid, it is inevitable that the business will demand that disruption and productivity loss be minimised.
- The willingness of the organisation to support the financial investment potentially needed for implementing a PPM software tool-set will be a major issue, and tool selection is often fraught with technical difficulties. 'Rip-and-replace' solutions come at a high price – cultural, technical and financial. The adoption of PPM will need to take into account the impact on existing processes and systems. Will they be replaced? If so, why, and at what cost to the business? Integration, flexibility and configurability will determine the successful choice of any PPM solution.
- It is simply human nature that people will blame the tools and processes to hide their own lack of knowledge and understanding. All tools and processes are created with their own set of idiosyncrasies; it will therefore be important to provide continual support and training. However, you must be prepared to accept that no matter how much you train, hand-hold, and evangelise, some people will simply not understand PPM.

- In order for the executive levels to get a bird's-eye view of information on multiple projects, it is essential that the business be able to collect that information and to determine who is working on what. One of the most crucial but often overlooked barriers to PPM is the adoption of timesheet technology as a method of collecting baseline information. It is essential to manage the 'Big Brother Syndrome' – the suspicion that the business is only using timesheet technology to keep tabs on the staff. Instead, it is necessary to sell the benefits of increased employee visibility, utilisation and productivity.

2.4 Best practice considerations – who, why, what, how and when

Before we delve deeper into the practical application of PPM there are several best practice issues that need to be highlighted. Any organisation thinking of PPM should strongly consider using these while deploying PPM.

2.4.1 Who: engaging the right people

In order to organise the business for PPM, senior management and executive buy-in is absolutely critical – without this, PPM will fail. Executive sponsorship is essential to create awareness, provide support, build consensus and motivate stakeholders at all levels to participate effectively. Executive sponsorship gives PPM the all-important 'nod' from above.

2.4.2 Why: identifying the pain and calculating the ROI

Justifying PPM within any organisation depends on the business's ability to sell PPM's benefits. This can be achieved by conducting a health check to establish key areas of pain and then to dovetail this with an ROI model. Ownership of the health check and ROI model should be with the key project stakeholders and executive sponsors. The ROI analysis will help the organisation define and quantify potential top-line benefits and also identify the quantitative and qualitative benefits from deploying PPM, such as in revenue, market capitalisation, increased customer base and decreased attrition.

2.4.3 What: selecting the right tools

The successful deployment of PPM will critically depend on selection of the right software tools, and a key determinant is how the tools integrate with the rest of the business from both the cultural and the technical viewpoints. As discussed earlier, when selecting PPM tools the organisation should look to avoid a 'rip-and-replace' tool-set. It is essential to choose tools that are scalable and flexible, avoiding excessive and restrictive customisation, and above all, that integrate with peripheral applications and are able to evolve as the business evolves. Successful tool selection needs to be embraced by everyone in the organisation, and if an application is too difficult to use, or requires people to make drastic changes to the way they do their job, then PPM will fail.

2.4.4 How: testing the tools and processes

Deploying a proof of benefit (PoB) is an essential prerequisite that enables the organisation to minimise all the risks associated with the implementation of a change project like PPM. The PoB provides an actual 'real-world' view of the value of a PPM solution within a 'low risk' environment and is an excellent way to facilitate the communication of potential return on investment (ROI) and return on opportunity (ROO). The PoB is in actuality the first deliberate step in a phased approach to implementation by starting small and then rolling out more functionality and coverage over time.

2.4.5 When: avoiding 'big bang' deployment

It is essential to understand that PPM by its very nature is a change project and that each business is different in terms of its level of maturity and ability to handle change. Building on a PoB as part of a larger, phased approach should be undertaken and this should be based on the company's internal project management readiness and maturity. Use the results of your business case and PoB to scale the PPM solution throughout those areas of the business that are most needy. An incremental implementation allows cultural issues to be solved on a domain-by-domain level and then its success to be sold upwards throughout the organisation. PoB allows the business to cultivate best practice examples that can be converted into quantifiable results for management.

In summary, get senior sponsorship; identify an area within the business with the greatest business need; health-check its requirements; build a proof of benefit (PoB); report back ROI, and have a phased deployment from one business areas to another. PPM implementation will be more successful and will minimise risks with a personalised, incremental approach because rapid wins foster greater sponsorship and momentum.

PART II

Prepare and organise for Project Portfolio Management

We have defined PPM as a method in which the business manages its projects as a series of investments. We have also stated that PPM is about ensuring that the business has the right balance of projects, focused on taking the organisation where it needs to go.

We now turn our attention to the practical application of PPM by exploring how the business can start to organise itself for the deployment of PPM.

It is essential to understand that if the business's projects, programmes and portfolios are to be synchronised, these have to be supported with implementation of the right staffing, tools and processes.

Successful implementation requires rigour, process adherence and a level of technology, together with cultural and practical support from the organisation's leaders. There is no 'one size fits all' and the approach can be tailored to the differing needs of each organisation. However, when the business is looking at deploying PPM, there are some basic common issues that need to be addressed.

Here are the core issues which Part II will focus on:

- *Executive sponsorship*: PPM is fundamentally a top-down process reliant on executive and senior management sponsorship. We argue that executive leaders need to take ownership of PPM, manage it as a change project and sell its benefits to board level.
- *The Project Portfolio Management Team (PPMT) and the Programme Management Office (PMO)*: We explore why it is best practice to create a PMO as a means of centralising best practice techniques and to coordinate this 'project knowledge centre' with the PPMT. We pay particular attention to the relationship between the PMO and the PPMT and explain how they differ in role and function. We advocate the deployment of a PPMT that enables executive and senior management to buy into the PPM idea as well as providing for basis for

communicating project information upstream and downstream within the business via the PMO.

- *Role based visibility*: We look at how to empower the relevant project stakeholders within the business through the implementation of role based visibility, that is, through software dashboards. We emphasise how role based visibility provides a fast and effective means of integrating the strategic with the operational, enabling the business to drill through layers of management in order to manage project milestones, resources capability, budget allocation and so on, as well as keeping close tabs on project progress.
- *Real-time component*: We examine the notion of the 'real-time enterprise' and how it is essential for enabling project based enterprises to make quicker and more accurate decisions about their business's projects. We explore the practical application of 'real time' by taking an example of a real-time information inhibitor – the widely used spreadsheet. We examine why it is essential to move away from user-centric desktop client applications and adopt web based applications to deliver better project management and collaboration.
- *Governance framework*: We will look at the importance of corporate governance, why the issue of accountability is essential to PPM, and how the implementation of milestone management is essential to making projects more transparent to stakeholders.
- *Resource capability*: We then move on to examine why it is essential that your PPM implementation be able to have a complete real-time view of the business's resources in order to deliver on project demands.
- *The PPM tool-set*: We then delve into an examination of the key technical issues involved when selecting a PPM tool-set, and also give a detailed technical breakdown of such a tool-set's key features and capabilities.
- *Building the PPM framework*: Within this section we explore in detail the mechanics of the PPM framework and argue that management of an effective PPM structure is about the selection and prioritisation of projects to deliver the highest value, based on the pre-established portfolio business definition, criteria and infrastructure.
- *Kick-starting the PPM process*: Finally we look at how the process can be kick-started. We discuss in detail both the requirements capture and vendor selection processes, then we map out the low risk, high value deployment model in the form of a PoB. We argue that the PoB allows the organisation to synergise, by trial and error, tool selection with 'people and process build' in a low risk environment without adversely impacting business-as-usual activities or incurring the political fallout and cost of a problematic software implementation.

CHAPTER 3

Organise the business for PPM

3.1 Building PPM leadership through executive sponsorship

Executive radars are typically focused on the following concerns and issues:

- What contribution is each specific project making to corporate objectives?
- How do the costs and ROI compare with similar project investments?
- Are we maximising on the investments generated by our projects, products, assets and resources?
- In what areas should we focus our project investments and resources for maximum competitive advantage?
- Should we kill any existing projects and reprioritise investment elsewhere within the business?
- Do we have the right mix of low, medium and high project investments?
- What resources do we need to complete each project as planned?
- Do we have resources in place to accomplish business projects?
- What is the status of each project and programme?
- What is the history of schedule prediction vs performance?

Executives are more accountable today for answering these questions than ever before, and are under the critical eye of the shareholders and the board to deliver value, maximising ROI while minimising the risks.

It is at this level, that of the 'executive community', that buy-in and sponsorship are paramount. The executive decision making stream is critical to the success or failure of any project and establishing a PPM process and solution within the business is only workable if it has executive support and visibility. And this support is only tenable in the long term if members of the executive body have a reliable and workable framework for extracting the information they need.

PPM is a lame duck if executives and senior management do not take ownership and are unable to sell its benefits to board level. Executive sponsorship provides the infrastructure whereby the right authority is empowered to drive the right behaviour in the organisation. In other words, a truly strategic approach to deploying PPM must start at the top in order for accountability, transparency and above all credibility to extend throughout the organisation.

It is essential that the establishment of PPM within the business be based on upon a simple yet effective premise of managing it as a *change project* from the top down. Executives can eliminate many problems simply by involving themselves at the appropriate points in the project delivery process, and this is never more true than with the implementation of PPM.

Moreover, the tools and processes that are put in place must be bolstered by continual executive support and not delegated downwards once the process has been implemented. Therefore, as discussed in the next section, a permanent executive place on the PPMT is not only required but is essential to its long term longevity.

Managing the PPM process from the top down increases visibility of the primary project planning functions, enabling executives to make top-level decisions that are based on coherent factual information, presented and accessed simply and delivered in real time. This visibility gives the executive decision making stream a bird's-eye view of each department, their project progress, their cost and who is responsible for each. As a result, executives are able to make strategic and operational decisions quickly which can be adjusted as changes to projects in the pipeline arise.

The strategic contents of the portfolio, reasons for selection and execution fall to executive champions and project sponsors. However, as stated earlier, the successful deployment of the PPM process is in effect a multi-layered relationship and is also dependent on how executive and strategic decisions about the business portfolio of projects are translated in real time to the operational side of the business. In other words, how does the business communicate downstream with its programme, project and resources managers? It is simply not enough for both sides to communicate within the strategic planning process, then afterwards for the focus to split back to each side's respective interests with no iterative communication between the two elements.

A key component of sponsorship by executives is their role in managing PPM deployment as a change management project. In other words, change management needs to be represented at board level and executive buy-in will be needed to help set up a change programme that will address the cultural issues stirred up by PPM. The change programme will need to agree a corporate vision and justify the necessary resource management decisions needed to select, buy and implement the PPM tools. Executive sponsorship will provide the PPM process with the necessary leadership to drive its implementation, weed out resistance, and sell its benefits to the board as well as provide it with long term sustainability and credibility. As PPM is pushed down to the lower levels of an organisation, this will begin to change the culture and impact the way of doing business. Next we explore how executive sponsorship is embedded within the PPM process and how this is then distilled throughout the business via the Project Portfolio Management Team (PPMT) and the Programme Management Office (PMO).

3.2 Organising the PPMT

Imagine the following scenario:

> IT are measuring the wrong things, they are spending too much time with maintenance and support, and prioritising projects based on which users are most vocal. Consequently, IT are reinforcing wrong behaviours for both developers and users.

Project Portfolio Management is designed to correct this by the governance and alignment of resources and investments with corporate goals. Governance simply means good, transparent decision making, and improving project governance is accomplished by accurately communicating current and future project performance to management in real time. Alignment is about the contribution of business projects to strategic objectives. Improved alignment is accomplished by better defining and communicating the business's strategy and encouraging behaviour that contributes to the achievement of that strategy by specifying what is really important in the different business units of the company. Therefore central to PPM governance and alignment, as well as providing a structured environment for deciding which projects are important to the business, is the creation of a PPMT.

What is the nature of the PPMT and what is its precise role within the PPM process? The PPMT has two primary roles, which can be defined as follows:

- The PPMT is accountable for the management of the entire project portfolio process. For example, the PPMT is responsible for:
  - building the project portfolio registry

- o interpreting and applying strategic objectives
- o selecting, categorising, funding and prioritising
- o managing and reviewing the portfolio
- The PPMT acts as the main intersection point between the strategic decision making level, that is, the board, and the operational level, that is, the PMO. It is within the PPMT that the executive sponsor will cultivate the relationships within which to deliver and sustain the PPM process.

The PPMT defines and develops a detailed, continuous process by which projects are evaluated, prioritised, selected, and managed. Its primarily responsibilities can be broken down as follows:

- initiating project ideas and proposals
- ensuring that the overall project portfolio stays aligned with business objectives
- ensuring individual projects are aligned with global strategy
- establishing executive sponsors and communicating portfolio status to the board
- feeding back portfolio status to the PMO and other relevant project stakeholders
- enforcing a collaborative effort that enables senior PPMT leaders to reach agreement on portfolio objectives
- providing coaching and training to PPMT members to help them to understand portfolio evaluation criteria and to enable them to efficiently generate inputs to the portfolio process
- evaluating, accepting or rejecting new project proposals, accelerating and decelerating existing projects, allocating resources, and continuously managing the portfolio pipeline over time
- communicating to the PPMT, the PMO and the board which projects are approved and prioritised
- verifying project cost, strategic value, and risks
- adjudicating resource conflicts between projects, building 'what if' scenarios and modelling business capability
- recommending resource allocations for final approval by senior team members
- maintaining visibility of key project information across the enterprise
- identifying lessons learned and continually refining the portfolio management process
- establishing analytical and scoring criteria such as score cards, earned value analysis, cost/benefit analysis, and so on

- providing, via the PMO, detailed time reports, expense reports, budgets and financial information in order to ensure that decisions are based on tangible and factual data
- gaining access to operational reporting, to augment its analysis and ensure that it presents the right options to business leaders
- providing access dashboards which enable users to create, edit and share information with other users

Via the PMO, the PPMT has access to a variety of supply streams including resource functionality and data (including skills and schedule), project details (schedule, budgets, issues, risks, and so on), related documents, discussion threads and recent approvals, as well as opportunity management (pricing models, schedules, and so on) in order to make the right decisions for the business.

In summary, not only does the PPMT manage the portfolio process, but it is also intended to support core programme and project management related functions including scope management, baseline change management, project scheduling, resource management, cost management and project reviews. The PPMT provides the forum in which the organisation is able to bring together the business's full complement of projects, their related resource needs and allocations, risks, benefits, schedules, issues and scope. In addition, the PPMT provides a *global analytical view* of the dependencies in relation to the business's programmes and projects, and allows the relevant managers to balance deliverables to get the most benefit from their projects.

As can be seen from Figure 7, typical roles within the PPMT include those of:

- *PPMT sponsor*: C-level and/or executive sponsor who has P&L and cap-ex spend responsibility and who is also able to champion the portfolio management process at board level
- *PPMT leader*: the evangelist who is responsible for spearheading PPM within the business and has one of the most important roles within the PPMT alongside the executive sponsor. This person is focused on leading the management team behind PPM and has overall responsibility for managing delivery of the portfolio process and communicating its performance to both business strategic and operational functions. The PPMT leader is responsible for providing and updating (for example, in response to changing strategy) the value judgments and policy decisions needed to guide the team. The PPMT leader should have the ability to influence decisions to suspend, at any time,

further commitment of investment monies due to failure to make anticipated progress, changing economic climates, or shifts in business objectives

- *Functional advocate*: represents a key department, unit or business function, their focus being on ensuring that the interests of their domain are fairly reflected within the portfolio management process
- *Project advocate*: is focused on best practice in terms of project delivery and project team competence. Their role is to help communicate the reason why a project exists, understand both the high-level and the low-level picture, benefits and ROI, and have the ear of an executive stakeholder as regards project priority
- *PMO*: a critical support stream for the PPMT (see Figure 8), with the PMO leader representing the PMO team and being focused on instilling best practice methodologies and standards so as to control planning practices and project management techniques. The PMO produces reports and analysis, and distributes to the PPMT all project information and associated interdependencies, including objectives, milestones, budgets, project priority level and stages of the project life cycle

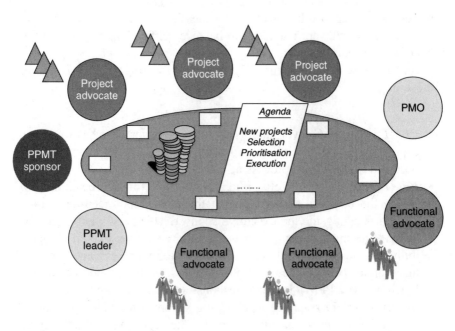

Figure 7 Roles within the PPMT

Portfolio needs	PMO provides
• Management commitment	• Information, education
• Effective decision making	• Data, scenarios, process
• Expert project managers	• Facilitation, coaching
• Motivated community	• Leadership, passion
• Sustainable practices	• Rigour, standards

Figure 8 PMO and PPMT support streams

We now turn to exploring the relationship between the PPMT and the PMO. In section 3.3, we will see how PPM assists the project management process, via the Programme Management Office, to:

- *plan and monitor in real time*: presenting a current real-time view of the state of progress and interdependencies between projects
- *manage risks, issues, and change control*: ensuring that the impact of external events is assessed and assimilated into the projects affected
- *monitor quality and financial control*: enabling performance to be demonstrated and budgets secured
- *enhance stakeholder communications*: ensuring that relevant stakeholder groups are kept aware of progress and are consulted before any major changes are undertaken

3.3 Supporting PPM with a PMO

Realising the true potential of a PMO has always been problematic. According to a KPMG survey, few PMOs provide any kind of strategic support vehicle for pushing project governance through the organisation's entire project portfolio.

The KPMG survey cites the following as hindering the potential of PMOs:

- PMO resourced with generalists/administrators (42 per cent claim the majority have predominantly operational skills)
- lack of formal project management qualifications (only 24 per cent claim this represents the majority of their project managers)
- informal processes for developing project manager competency (only 42 per cent adopt formal processes)
- PMO leadership lacking in strong business acumen and commercial training

What is the role of the PMO? What is its relationship with the PPMT and the project management process? How can the true potential of the PMO be realised? A project manager is a very different animal to a programme manager. However, the relationship within the business is designed to be mutually complementary. This is also true of the relationship between the PMO and the PPMT.

Delivering complex programmes on time and on budget is a major challenge for any organisation. With diverse but interrelated projects, resources, and processes, conflicts are inevitable and success is often elusive. The biggest challenges facing most organisations today are having the ability to know which of their projects are in trouble at any given time, and how they will get them back on track. With information and people so widely distributed, the critical ability to check project status and proactively identify problems can be next to non-existent. Moreover this is also compounded by disparate levels of project management knowledge, skills, abilities, techniques and methodologies from one business unit and department to another.

Disparate information and poor communication about project interdependencies typically result in:

- *project delays*: projects run late and do not deliver the desired results
- *no standardised method*: typically, many organisations have no centralised or enterprise-wide project management method, resulting in fragmented and ad hoc compliance to project governance standards and procedures
- *resource bottlenecks*: key resources are chronically overscheduled and there is no clear method for project managers to get the right people for their projects
- *out-of-control costs*: redundant projects are occurring in different business lines and are costing the organisation more than estimated
- *insufficient information*: management has little or no insight into what projects are being undertaken, or how well they are being carried out
- *no decision framework*: projects are undertaken with little or no analysis, with projects having a strong champion or determined evangelist driving other possible investments out of consideration

Therefore businesses that want to improve project outcomes as well as provide critical project information for executives, or institute an analytical project decision process, are turning to the creation of a PMO – a means of managing projects within an enterprise environment.

As defined in Chapter 1, programme management is the process of managing multiple, ongoing, interdependent projects. The PMO provides a layer above the project management process, focusing on selecting the best group of programmes, defining them in terms of their constituent projects and providing an infrastructure whereby projects can be run successfully while leaving the job of delivery to the project management community.

The focus of the PMO is to coordinate and communicate on all programmes and projects in the enterprise, as well as to be the knowledge centre (see Figure 9) with regard to training, leadership, mentoring, best practice, project governance standards, and so on that supports managers in the implementation of the tasks and work packages required to achieve successful project completion.

Figure 9 The PMO as the knowledge centre

Aspect	Programme management	Project management
Focus	Process to create deliverables	Deliverables
Scope	Multi-project and interdependencies	Single project
Communication	Among projects	Within a project
Organisation	Project/Programmes office	Project team

Figure 10 Differences between programme and project management

Figure 10 shows the main differences between programme management and project management.

The PMO's role within the business is not only to act as a knowledge centre, but also to help marry project management process with the executive streams by working closely with the PPMT. This relationship is designed to help the business to identify the precise measures that need to be taken in order to turn strategic goals into reality, as well as to determine the key performance indicators that show whether goals are being met.

Project Portfolio Management

The PMO provides the necessary overview and coordination to deliver projects on time and on budget by managing and reporting on schedules, risks, costs, quality, scope and resources across all projects. At the heart of a PMO is its relationship with the PPMT, the aim being to enable the business to coordinate and integrate complex multi-project initiatives across an entire enterprise. This partnership between the PMO and the PPMT is there to empower the executive decision making stream with the necessary information to help prioritise and balance project initiatives, justify decisions, measure risk vs return and allocate resources in a way that maximises their impact on the business.

One of the main issues when implementing a PPM process is that different layers of management within the business have their own territorial issues and perspectives. As stated earlier, the PPMT consists of executives and senior postholders who are charged with responsibility for making all key decisions that affect the project portfolio.

As can be seen from Figure 11, the PMO provides the bridge that joins the operational stream with the strategic stream. The PMO is a body of senior project stakeholders and managers that has responsibility for managing all the business's projects from an operational perspective as well as reporting back to the PPMT on their outcome (see Figure 12).

By centralising overall operational responsibility for all the organisation's projects in the PMO, a complete picture of project activity can be painted. The PPMT is able to utilise the tactical structure of the PMO to collect all the necessary 'coal face information' to manage and evaluate the health of the business's projects.

The formation of a PMO is not only designed to drive top-down accountability; it also supports the complete operational framework for managing

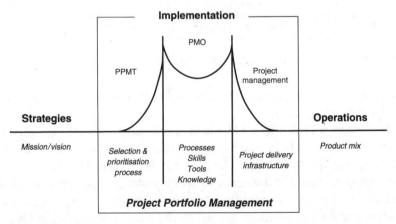

Figure 11 Bridging the operational and strategic divide with a PMO

Aspect	Project Portfolio Management (PPM)	Programme management	Project management
Focus	Deliverables linked to strategic objectives	Process to create deliverables	Deliverables
Scope	Selects, prioritises and optimises entire project portfolio	Multi-project and interdependencies	Single project
Communication	Across the business	Among projects	Within a project
Organisation	PPMT	PMO	Project team

Figure 12 PPM, programme and project management relationship model

a multi-project environment. In effect a PMO is an information repository that provides the visibility needed to understand the health of ongoing projects and the potential impact of planned projects – and ensures that all projects are evaluated in the same manner. Without a PMO 'knowledge centre', executives and the PPMT are hindered in their ability to make the necessary collective decisions based on the right information.

The PMO therefore assumes two key roles, depending on which needs of the organisation are being served:

- *Tactical*: The PMO provides direct support to projects in several areas such as scope management, baseline change management, project scheduling, resource management, cost management and project reviews. The PMO provides the information required for decision making and ensures that the decisions are being carried out.
- *Strategic*: The PMO supports the PPM framework, which in addition supports project prioritisation, performance management and benefits realisation (see Figure 13). The PPMT intersects with the executive stream, allowing the organisation to make strategic 'go/kill/hold/fix' decisions on key projects in the context of managing a balanced portfolio of investments.

In summary, the PMO is the function responsible for coordinating, planning, overseeing and monitoring an organisation's multi-project environment. Through the PPM process the PMO enforces executive accountability and transparency by connecting the organisation's projects to the business's portfolio strategic decision making stream. The information supplied by the PMO flows directly into the PPMT's funding, selection, prioritisation and resourcing processes.

PMOs are becoming a standard feature within many organisations and are viewed as the operational centre supporting any project within the business. They act as the clearing house for project information and the

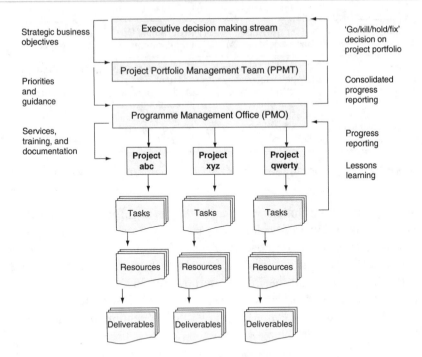

Figure 13 Board, PPMT, PMO and project hierarchy

driving force for project delivery. The main specific responsibilities of the PMO include:

- *Project management, control, delivery and alignment*:
  - monitoring project outcomes and communicating this upstream to the PPMT and downstream to project managers
  - increasing communication and coordination across projects
  - advising the PPMT on the benefits and status of projects
  - advising and reporting on the placement of new and elimination of old projects
  - endorsing, advising and supporting project managers
  - confirming successful delivery and sign-off at the closure of the projects
  - managing resource utilisation across the organisation as a whole, matching project needs with specialised skills and availability
  - ensuring critical projects are on time and within budget by providing objective accountability and review at every stage, from initiation to closure
  - using dashboards to enhance the roles of project and programme managers within the enterprise

- *Financial accounting*:
  - o assisting project managers with budget control
  - o maintaining financial status reports on all projects
  - o analysing interfaces and critical cost dependencies between projects and recommending appropriate action
  - o maintaining a list of stakeholders and their financial interests
- *Project management support*:
  - o providing a single point of contact for all project information
  - o training, coaching, guidance and mentoring
  - o developing and holding project templates and master copies of all project and programme information
  - o generating all necessary quality management documentation
  - o maintaining, controlling and updating documentation
  - o establishing and maintaining an electronic registry of project information for use by both the PPMT and project managers
- *Methodologies, standards and metrics*:
  - o guardianship of project methodologies (for example, Prince2), standards and metrics
  - o compiling reports and collecting information from project reviews
  - o providing a central, customer focused office to care for the concerns of the client, sponsor and project stakeholders
  - o providing assistance to the PPMT in selecting and analysing projects
  - o establishing consistent practices and standards for programme governance arrangements, including project planning, reporting, change control, analysing risks and maintaining and updating the risk register

The relationship between the business, the portfolio, programmes, projects and work packages can be best defined as shown in Figure 14.

3.4 Embedding project governance within a PPM process

According to a KPMG survey, compliance drivers have been in a significant public spotlight globally. The Sarbanes-Oxley Act of 2002, International Financial Reporting Standards (IFRS), Basel II and a host of multinational, industry-specific or local governance and regulatory requirements (for example, within the UK, the Gershon Efficiency Agenda) have contributed to increased focus on project activity and governance.

Level	Role
Board	Takes a holistic view of the enterprise, defines and controls the enterprise strategy and ensures consistency throughout.
Portfolio	Has access to company strategy, goals and vision, which will become key objectives at the programme, project and work package levels. Gains a holistic view of the progress and status of all the company's projects and programmes, and gauges the level of benefit realisation being achieved against strategic objectives. Manages the project selection and prioritisation process and has responsibility for managing the project pipeline.
Programmes	Defines, establishes and manages the groups of interdependent projects and programmes, as well as gaining visibility of progress within the individual projects and work packages. Programme managers, project managers/administrators and project sponsors use this level to help define, establish and implement best practice project management from concept to implementation.
Projects	Project managers and project teams will use this level to set up and manage projects either independently or as part of a programme. Gives project managers clear visibility of the progress of their project's work packages.
Work packages	Gives visibility of individual tasks and work packages, that is, the component parts of the project.

Figure 14 Relationship between the business, the portfolio, programmes, projects and work packages

Laws like the Sarbanes-Oxley Act, Basel II and the Companies Bill have presented considerable challenges for corporations in the UK, Europe and North America. With corporate responsibility and the need for governance high in the public's and media's eyes, there has been much discussion regarding how the management of the corporate projects and resource pool needs accurately to reflect contemporary business needs and to deliver the services required to support the organisation's activities.

For example, the Sarbanes-Oxley Act of 2002, enacted to bolster investor confidence following the scandals surrounding the failures of Enron and other major corporations, contains strict regulations designed 'to protect investors by improving the accuracy and reliability of corporate disclosures'. Sarbanes-Oxley requires, for example, visibility of key strategic metrics that support alignment with organisational performance management, as well as operational statements linked to dynamic business and project plans that can highlight anomalies and provide workflow to ensure awareness and action. In essence, legislation like Sarbanes-Oxley ultimately demands that corporate executives be responsible for establishing, maintaining and implementing sound internal governance controls and procedures. Sarbanes-Oxley has therefore been a catalyst for the development of the discipline of information technology governance since the early 2000s, which has now spilled over into other parts of the business, with demands for greater project accountability.

Project governance standards form a subset of corporate governance standards. The rising interest in them within PPM is not only due to compliance initiatives as stated above, but also acknowledges that projects can easily get out of control and profoundly affect the performance of an organisation. The project governance process is essentially about building an accountability framework to encourage best practice behaviour in the project delivery process. The main goals of project governance are to ensure that the organisation's projects generate business value and that the business is able to mitigate the risks that are associated with the delivery process. Project governance therefore brings together into a single organisational decision making framework all internal and external groups involved in the project decision making process, including:

- Board of directors
- Senior executives
- Managers
- Workers
- Shareholders
- Regulators
- Customers
- Suppliers

The project governance process is designed to distribute various types and levels of responsibility among these various project stakeholders, relevant to their position within the business, in order to ensure best practice project delivery. It is designed to embed accountability and provide a balanced approach to understanding where, when, and why a project has failed, gone out of control or not been delivered according to plan.

We discuss many of the important elements of good project governance throughout the book. However, here is a checklist of some of the most typical:

- project business case development, stating the objectives of the project and specifying scope, and so on
- development of project plans that span initiation through to development and delivery
- maintenance of systems to assess compliance of the completed project with its original objectives
- identification of all stakeholders with an interest in the project and establishment of a defined method of communication with each stakeholder

- development of an agreed specification for the project deliverables
- assignment of project related roles and responsibilities
- maintenance of a central project document repository
- maintenance of a central resource repository
- provision of a process for the management and resolution of issues
- provision of a process for the recording and communication of risks
- maintenance of standards for quality review of the key governance document

Project governance can be determined by the business's level of project management maturity; each individual business will shape its governance process around its own organisational needs and structures. You will see that many of the project governance elements outlined above will find their way into the PPM process as it is rolled out. In fact PPM is a formalised method of implementing a governance process by putting together a selection and prioritisation that ensures that all projects contribute to the organisation's strategic objectives. However, embedding project governance within the PPM process is underpinned by three critical determinants:

- formulation of a two-way governance and accountability contract between the business and the project delivery process
- the speed and reliability with which the business's project delivery information is accessed and administered to the business
- how the business fuses these together and tracks the project delivery process via milestone management

Governance and accountability within the PPM process are embodied in a series of controls and procedures underpinned by a two-way contract between the business and the project stakeholders. In order for the project management process to deliver, it needs to be supplied with the relevant tools, assets, budget and resources. These need to be agreed with and supplied by the business; without this agreement the project management process cannot justifiably undertake to guarantee timely and successful completion of the business's project portfolio. When supplied and armed with the relevant tools to do the job, the project management process needs to be held accountable for its delivery. As we will discuss later in this section, milestone management forms the base structure of this contract.

All businesses need to provide credible evidence that their management of resources, programmes and projects is in line with regulatory requirements and project governance standards. Over recent years there has been a rapid development of the techniques and processes needed to fulfil this information compliance and governance requirement. Large blue chip enterprises have implemented planning and resourcing capabilities which tie in to year-end reporting and financial systems, helping measure past performance. The consensus of opinion is that this reporting one to three months after a project has ended is not good enough. The glaring hole in this approach is the lack of visibility of project activities at the coal face as they happen. Business information about projects, resources and capability should be seen from a 'lights on now' perspective, not from a 'historical' perspective. Today's enterprises need to understand project progress and business needs as they are right now – not as they were three months ago.

Gaining and managing the visibility of the rapidly changing environment of a project is the key to implementing a PPM process. The typical project management processes will make reference to the project in terms of:

- time, schedules, resource utilisation, costs and scope
- single users, project teams and/or departments

While these items are certainly key elements of PPM and are of significant importance, they are not the topics on the typical executive radar screen. Rather than the traditional 'When will the project be finished and what will it cost?', the executive stream is focused on how projects are contributing to a larger set of strategic objectives and what the impact will be today, not several months down the line. Moreover, executives are also focused on how this accountability and project governance are translated and detailed throughout the organisation. With the implementation of PPM, executives are as it were 'articulating a different language'.

The PPM project governance process needs to be tied into a relevant role based structure in order to ensure that information is easily rolled up and down the business, linking the executive and operational levels. This is designed to give business managers and decision makers a far more accurate and up-to-date view of their information and of the business. Communication and visibility are at the heart of a successful project governance process, enabling the business to maintain a consistent view of the project portfolio throughout the length and breadth of the organisation. Not only is it essential that project success be embedded in the organisation's overall strategic objectives, but it is crucial that the latter be communicated so that everyone across the organisation understands the business's corporate goals and decision making process. Also, it is essential that the relevant stakeholders are made accountable for their role within the project delivery process.

Understanding the strategy at all levels of the organisation is essential because even simple and seemingly non-strategic decisions are affected. Managers at all levels of the organisation need to use strategic objectives as a guide for ongoing operational decisions. A clear line of communication helps define the expected outcomes and answers.

Project governance naturally follows from a formalised decision making infrastructure for managing the business's portfolio of projects. However, the relationship between governance and projects is not only about the organisation's ability to monitor project activity, but also about the need to have a single consistent system. Too often executives are not only horrified to find that projects are not doing what they want them to do, but they are also unable to interrogate systems and processes that will give them a single version of the truth.

Although the framework for governance initiatives varies, most organisations will need to look to develop a unified decision making structure and technical process that:

- defines how project investment decisions will be made
- identifies where accountability lies for those decisions
- monitors accountability
- makes it possible to use this process to improve the management of the resulting projects

Effective project governance within PPM requires a system that ensures that decisions are made the same way up and down the organisation and by the right people. Central to driving organisational accountability and business performance is the deployment of 'enterprise-wide milestone management'. This is essential to increase awareness of milestones and also the importance of achieving them both with senior management and with team members.

Milestones underpin the delivery of products, services and benefits to an organisation. Their visibility to management is in relation to project and programme control, not just for project based staff but also for the business stakeholders (such as account managers, directors and the board). Milestone management is central to controlling what the business has agreed to deliver both internally and to customers; however, the reporting of milestones, as with any other reporting, can be cumbersome when attempted at different levels in the management hierarchy. It is therefore critical to deploy a PPM process that make these milestones visible to all levels of management, embodied within a single integrated system and sourced from a single database.

For example, let us say that one of the high-level objectives is to increase the customer base. This can be broken down into multiple capabilities, for example, CRM system improvements, customer segmentation and a promotion scheme. These high-level capabilities can be broken down into programmes and the multiple projects that make up the CRM programme, for example, to upgrade software (IT Department), market research (Marketing Department), customer loyalty campaign (Sales and Marketing Department), and so on.

Progress against milestones needs to be monitored within a single integrated system, and full support throughout all levels of the business should be given to project changes that will enable milestones to be achieved. It is recommended that organisations have one central view of all projects against key milestones, rather than relying on a number of ad hoc and/or stand-alone systems, as this greatly improves project and milestone visibility. This single integrated system and process remedies governance and accountability very easily because it provides for one version of the truth and a single point of entry. The system and processes need to be designed to make project information consistent, current and complete, and also to ensure that staff work only within this single solution and according to clearly defined processes, eliminating the time it takes to move between applications and manage multiple workflows. Rather than solely managing project delivery from the task upwards, as with many traditional project management processes, it is essential to set a governance-style contract, that is, to agree milestones with the project managers that distils accountability from the top down. In other words, as we outlined earlier, on the one hand, project managers are accountable for their deliverables, while on the other, executives are accountable for ensuring that they provide the necessary resources and elements to achieve these deliverables. Moreover, it is essential that executives and the project manager alike are able to see in real time whether projects are on time, why have they been moved and who moved them, and the impact that this has on the business as a whole. One of the primary advantages of this framework is that it helps participants at the negotiating table to separate the map from the territory and safeguard against decisions that may be short-sighted or that may be driven by the individual that wields the largest proverbial hammer. It ensures that business leaders are better able to spot project redundancies, resource appropriately, and understand budget allocation and spend, as well as keeping close tabs on project progress.

Now we turn our attention to exploring in more detail some of the key components that are central to supporting the PPM project governance process, the PPMT and PMO functions, for example:

- role based dashboards as a means of enabling managers to perform root-cause analysis on the business projects delivery process
- implementation of a real-time information flow as a method by which project information can quickly flow between the various stakeholders to ensure that the changing nature of stakeholder needs and the environment in which the organisation operates get effectively factored into decision making processes
- implementation of a web based and centralised data system that ensures that all project information is accessed from a single source
- understanding of the business's ability to deliver on projects by gaining greater visibility and control of the organisation's resources.

3.5   Implementing enterprise-wide role based visibility

Maintaining consistent views of the business throughout an organisation can be a challenging task (see Figure 15).

Role	Challenges
CFO/CIO/CTO	• Cope with reduced budgets and increased expectations • Meet productivity goals consistently • Align business goals and projects • Use reliable measures to determine whether teams are really working on the 'right' projects • Put out fires and cut costs that prevent proactive planning
Portfolio/ Programme manager	• Prioritise initiatives, resources, and assets across the project portfolio • Assess and communicate portfolio, programme and project status • Identify and manage inter-project dependencies • Ensure consistent processes across projects • Optimise key resources across projects
Project / Resource manager	• Manage the project delivery process • Manage project outcomes and assess project status • Manage scope, planning, verification and change • Manage resource demand and supply • Maximise resource utilisation and minimise bench time
Team member	• Understand day-to-day project workloads • Input project timesheets and expenses • Access project documentation

Figure 15 Typical role based challenges

And yet it is critical that everyone in the organisation has the right information to help them focus on delivering on the same goals. A critical component of the successful deployment of PPM is ensuring that the relevant project information is visible to relevant people at the right time. Role based visibility via software dashboards is designed to provide visibility of the business's project activities at all levels within the organisation. Role based visibility is a major feature of most PPM software today; it offers metrics, alerting, drill-down and management capabilities to help the organisation as a whole monitor and understand project information in a simple format relevant to the role of each of the individual stakeholders. In other words, role based visibility provides the PPM process with an instant bird's-eye view of how key programmes, projects and initiatives at the operational level are impacting on the business's strategic roadmap. This method of distributing project data to a large and diverse set of roles within the business is typically outputted through a software dashboard interface, condensing large volumes of information, either to show the big picture or to present multiple dimensions simultaneously.

Deploying role based visibility ensures that business leaders are better able to spot project redundancies, resource projects appropriately, and understand budget allocation and spend, as well as keeping close tabs on project progress and how it impacts on the bottom line. But what is most important about role based visibility is the ability to deliver this information *in real time* and *on demand* from a centralised data source (see section 3.7). Role based visibility is a fast and effective means of integrating the strategic with the operational and providing a practical means of real-time opportunity detection.

It is simply not enough for the business to manage its projects at any one given level; visibility and responsibilities have to be distributed throughout the organisation. All types of roles must be able to view high-level data and also be able to quickly drill down into the details of a project.

Typical benefits derived from implementing role based visibility for individual project stakeholders are:

- Dashboards enable *executives* to gain high level 'P&L type visibility' of the project portfolio so they can quickly identify project investment status and risks.
- Dashboards enable *portfolio managers* to drill down from high-level portfolio views into detailed project data. For example, they provide them with 'what if' analysis in order to allow them to assess the impact of portfolio changes and roll this back up to assess the impact on the business.

- Dashboards give *programme and project managers* access to the tools they need to build task plans, find and schedule the most appropriately skilled staff resources, resolve issues, mitigate risks and track progress. Dashboards provide automated reporting and built-in notifications, meaning programme and project managers spend less time manually managing project documents and data and more time managing the delivery process.
- Dashboards provide *resource managers* with the ability to assess competing demands for resources and efficiently direct the right people to the most critical tasks and activities.
- Dashboards free *team members* from the randomising effects of shifting priorities and demands. Dashboards give team members instant assess to project tasks, workloads and activities and enable them to input timesheet and expense information.

A role based approach to PPM deployment is designed to bring rich and complex information direct to the desktop in a simple format relevant to the roles of key project coordinators and stakeholders. This level of communication and visibility allows executives and managers to gain an immediate grasp of the trends and relationships most significant to the business's performance data. In effect, not tailoring the process around a role based approach makes it virtually impossible to accelerate the time between getting information, understanding that information and, most importantly, acting on it. Where once executives and business leaders had to wait days or even weeks, with a role based approach to PPM the business is able to produce project performance reports, financial forecasting and resourcing needs in real time.

3.6 Creating real-time information flow

Poor access to real-time information is a key factor in why many businesses fail to react quickly enough to economic downturns, revenue shortfalls, missed earnings expectations, bankruptcies, corporate fraud, and so on. Not only do business leaders need to be able to predict the future shape of their markets, but they need access to real-time information that can enable the enterprise to be agile enough to cope with the sudden onset of unforeseeable business changes as well as unexpected opportunities.

Much has been written about the *real-time enterprise*. However, according to IT analysts Gartner, the concept is about:

> [an] organisation's ability to lever technology to reduce the gap between when data is recorded in a system and when it is available

for information processing. The idea is to get relevant information into the hands of decision-makers as soon as possible.

Moreover, Gartner go on to state that:

> We've been refining the same basic project management tools for 30 years. Yet people still have many project failures. People still somehow manage to report only at the very last minute that a project won't be finished on time.

Real-time information is therefore critical to anyone who manages complex, enterprise-wide, multi-project environments requiring quick decisions throughout all the levels of the business. For example, how quickly is your business able to make the following decisions?

- What mitigating action do we take if we go over budget?
- What action do we take when a vendor is late with a delivery?
- What happens if new government regulation impacts new product development?
- Do we have the capability to take on this new business?
- How fast can we modify the product roadmap to anticipate new market competition?

Here are the most typical *real-time information inhibitors* that hold back of successful project delivery:

- *Single-user-centric tools*: Many businesses are hindered because their planning and management information is locked into thousands of disparate single-user spreadsheets or client based project planning tools scattered across the enterprise. As we will explain later, spreadsheets are one of the mostly widely used but also widely abused applications and notoriously inaccurate and problematic when it comes to planning, resourcing and compiling management information.
- *Silos and isolated data*: Inside every organisation, whether it be in sales, finance or IT, individual units within the business have their own metrics and methods of analysing project status and performance. The reality is that data resides within a variety of domains which are physically as well as digitally scattered across wide areas of the enterprise. Rarely do these departments base their interpretations on the same data source, inhibiting not only the speed of decision making but more importantly its quality and accuracy.

- *Poor communication*: These disparate technical data infrastructures are the 'cancers' of corporate cultures. What emerge are isolated knowledge centres, little empires that are usually the preserve of middle managers, inaccessible to executives and team managers alike. Communication is therefore a roadblock between layers of management, preventing the business as a whole from detecting early warnings and opportunity signals.

Here are the key defining characteristics of a real-time enterprise, and the ways in which PPM has started to lever and utilise some of its key components:

- A defining characteristic of the real-time enterprise is corporate commitment and ability to distil corporate objectives throughout the organisation in a timely manner; in other words, senior management capability to translate corporate aims into practical operational object-ives and milestones. The PPM process levers the real-time component by making corporate, programme and project milestones visible to operational and seniors managers alike and updates these automatically as activity within the business takes place. At the operational level this also enables key personnel, such as resource and project managers, to track changes in real time (see section 3.4).
- Another key component of real-time information is the ability of the organisation to communicate with a wide range of stakeholders throughout the business, including internal employees as well as external business partners and investors. PPM utilises the real-time component via role based dashboards to ensure all stakeholders are informed as quickly as possible of events that are relevant to them. Role based technology is used to ensure stakeholders have the means to get appropriate information when it suits them and in formats they can use (see section 3.5).
- Real-time information delivery is frequently triggered by some kind of event that occurs in a business management application. A key component of PPM is access to a single, reliable data source that is updated from all areas of the business in real time. Access to a single data source ensures not only that no significant business event goes unnoticed by managers upstream and downstream within the business, but that there is also one single version of the truth (see this section).

PPM utilises the real-time component by providing the business with the ability to execute end-to-end project processes against set corporate strategies and objectives. As well as enabling the business to communicate in real time, project based information at every level delivers compelling value to customers and stakeholders both external and internal to the business.

As we have frequently stated one of the primary problems many businesses face is their inability to communicate and report project information upstream and downstream through layers of management. While top management are aware of strategic goals, most staff down the hierarchy typically have an alternative vision and little or no understanding of their obligation to support these goals because accurate information is simply not communicated. In effect the organisation builds, defines and displays information based on different interpretations of the strategy. The issue is compounded by reporting infrastructures that are typically fragmented, incomplete or linked to particular functions, with no means of centralising data into a coherent and meaningful system that management can trust. The result is that executives are spending days and weeks manually assembling project reports with data that is too often dangerously outdated by the time it reaches them. This acts as a filter, blurring the reality of project performance and leading to those nasty surprises that board members and investors so dislike. The end scenario is that executives and managers are unable to drive the organisation fast enough to meet the demands of sudden market changes.

An effective PPM system is critically determined by the implementation of a real-time system and process that articulates one single version of the truth; in other words, data that is held in one single database accessible via role based dashboards and is available on demand within a web environment. As organisations grow and change, they adopt and implement multiple systems and create a technical jungle of processes and solutions. The lack of a single standard prevents them working in a consistent environment, impacting management's ability to source real-time information, forcing decisions to be based on estimations or, at worst, guesswork. This inhibits executives and managers from spotting key operational bottlenecks, prevents them reducing risk exposure and making the necessary, faster, *information-rich* judgments on how to change and realise strategic outcomes.

The real-time component of PPM is designed to give an instant view of the performance of all programmes, projects and initiatives at both the operational and strategic levels. Just like role based visibility as mentioned earlier, the notion of real time ensures that business leaders are better able to manage project redundancies, resource appropriately, and understand budget allocation and spend, as well as keeping close tabs on project progress and how it impacts on the bottom line. Effective PPM is about putting the power of informed decision making information in the hands of the right manager in order to ensure that the enterprise is able to react in real time. Coupled with role based features, this creates employee accountability at all levels, pushing information to the desktop but only including the relevant information for each individual.

Essentially the real-time component *increases the visibility of primary business functions, enabling executives to make top-level decisions that are based on coherent factual information, presented and accessed simply and delivered on demand.* This visibility provided by real-time PPM gives executives a top-down insight into each department, their projects' progress, their cost and who is responsible for each. The single point of entry keeps information consistent, real-time and complete; this also ensures that the management team works within one solution, eliminating the time it takes to reconcile business intelligence from different points within the organisation.

3.7   Delivering a web based environment

When market conditions demand a rapid reaction and no real-time inform-ation is available, executives are forced to rely on educated guesswork and 'gut level' feeling. Why does this happen time and time again? The answer to this is simple – many organisations still build their processes around the adoption of user-centric and desktop-centric software applic-ations such as spreadsheets. Using spreadsheets to manage the project planning process and provide a means of reporting on project activity still remains the primary technology within most organisations today. Their use is largely attributable to the following:

- They come bundled on most users' desktop as part of a word processing office package.
- Ease of use and user-centric functionality mean they are easily adopted by the non-technical person.
- They are a cheap and cost-effective alternative to high priced planning and budgeting software.
- They are integrated with popular desktop project management applic-ations such as Microsoft Project.

Yet the history of project planning is plagued with the problems of relying on user-centric applications such as spreadsheets, largely because they are unable to articulate a single version of the truth. Using this type of 'technology' for project planning is in effect a semi-manual process which is slow, prone to error and extremely inflexible. The main problems with spreadsheets include:

- overdependence on key personnel
- version control and poor data quality
- lack of accountability, and a silo mentality
- lack of collaboration on and consolidation of users' work
- inflexibility in the face of structural and organisational changes
- inaccurate formulas
- poor modelling capabilities
- low data integrity
- inability to document formulas
- no real-time problem detection

Spreadsheets are not planning tools; they are simply screen oriented interactive programmes enabling a user to lay out predominantly finance based data. Such narrowly focused and error-prone tools simply do not permit organisations to alter plans, reforecast or modify project budgets in real time.

Albeit spreadsheets have enabled business users to create planning documents in a digital format that can be shared and updated, their user-centric focus limits their use as an effective planning tool. In our experience a single standard spreadsheet does not usually exist in any organisation. Instead, multiple types and versions are used to record time, schedule resources, forecast budgets and plan projects. Spreadsheets slow down the reporting cycle and do not provide for a dynamic capability to track milestones, 'what if' scenarios and workflow management. Typically managers find themselves spending more time administering the spreadsheet, and making sure none of the links and macros are broken, than managing the data and analysing it to ensure it fits the strategic plan.

With the advent of the internet, large enterprises have in recent years migrated from spreadsheet-dependent or desktop based software processes toward more sophisticated web based environments for planning, budgeting, and forecasting.

Since 2000, web based browser technology has taken another major step forward with the development of a new breed of technologies called Application Service Providers (ASPs). This means that mission-critical line-of-business project applications can now be delivered on demand anywhere in the world using a standard web browser. Now, instead of having a 'client footprint' application distributed across the enterprise, companies have a remote web based solution, allowing shared access anywhere across the organisation. These structures are maintained on a central web server rather than being dispersed across multiple users' desktops, and are crucial to embedding the real-time component within the PPM process. A web based infrastructure provides one single significant process advantage over its desktop predecessors – project and business information, including auditing and version control, is located and accessible at one central location. Web based infrastructure enables businesses to more quickly and reliably manage their project processes and base their decision making on more sophisticated and above all on more accurate data.

The key advantages to look for are:

- browser based, accessible from any type of computer without installing special software
- ease of access control, that is, both local to and remote from the business
- only one software installation/version to maintain
- low cost of ownership
- much more easily upgradeable than its desktop applications counterparts

We will explore in the following chapter the next generation of web based applications, the ASPs, and some of the practical advantages behind their deployment.

3.8   Deploying the centralised control of data

Companies that use spreadsheets, paper and manual processes, or multiple disconnected information systems that are loosely integrated, lack effective internal controls. These manual processes and loose integration points are control weaknesses that can lead to inaccurate, inconsistent or compromised data. Any reporting, analysis and decisions based on this poor data will be inaccurate and potentially harmful to the company, its executives and shareholders. The result is that executives are unable to drive the organisation fast enough and manipulate their project portfolios to meet the real-time demands of sudden market changes. Outdated information is compounded by the fact that departments behave like silos. Typically, many departments perform their planning and resourcing processes via fragmented semi-manual systems. For many organisations a single standard system does not exist and this lack of synergy prevents them from working in a consistent environment, ultimately impacting project performance.

Typical issues that businesses face with poor data control are:

- *Errors*: Spreadsheets, paper and manual processes are a poor corporate data store and are notoriously error-prone when managing multi-project environments.
- *Excessive paperwork*: Organisations waste days and weeks of management time reconciling multiple spreadsheets across different sources, often with conflicting views of project activity.
- *Dirty data*: Besides being extremely unwieldy for processes involving large volumes of data and multiple users, spreadsheets often contain substantial human errors and inconsistencies.
- *Poor communication*: Having financial data about your projects in a number of spreadsheets makes it hard to maintain one version of the truth.
- *No accountability*: Fragmented processes based on a spreadsheet model often result in project overspend and missed deadlines because they lack visibility of their strategy, plans, performance, and the cost of key projects.
- *Fragmented processes*: As mentioned above, the lack of a single process prevents the business from working in a consistent environment, impacting project performance.

A key philosophy driving effective PPM deployment is the obvious but often overlooked notion that data should be pooled into a centralised project repository. A centralised project repository is a source of information about the business's projects that can be accessed across the enterprise, which would typically include:

- business cases
- cost justifications
- basic project management data
- project metrics
- timelines
- dependencies
- resource assignments
- milestones
- deadlines
- deliverables

The PPM process needs to deliver real-time, data driven decisions, empowering senior management communication. The primary idea is to keep data consistent, get everyone working from the same source, and as a consequence enable the business to report project issues in real time. Key benefits include:

- *centralised planning*: overcoming project conflict and interpretation by integrating multiple projects into a single environment
- *accurate project data*: eliminating guesswork and 'grey zones' due to either inaccurate data, lost information or fragmented processes
- *online reporting*: accessing reports on detailed data that is critical for efficient project planning and management, in real time

3.9 Understanding your business's capability and resources

Here are three key questions about your business:

- Do you have a complete picture of the demands being made on the business?
- Do projects come from nowhere and do you have the capability to deliver on them?
- Are you able to quickly reprioritise resources?

Project driven organisations are often caught in a situation where project resource demands are coming at them from many different directions. Many organisations are simply ill-equipped to deal with these pressures. Rather than focusing on what is best for the business as a whole, managers are caught in a resource management game of cat and mouse. Many are forced to manage their resources via verbal networking and informal bartering. These informal processes limit the ability to optimise staffing levels, which inevitably leads to lower utilisation rates, skills shortages and lower profitability. Achieving an equitable balance between resource supply and project demand is a significant issue for successful management of the PPM process. The greatest problem for many is that they rely on home grown manual systems or numerous spreadsheets to achieve this. Such systems hamper the business, preventing it from:

- effectively assigning the right staff to the right job
- understanding whether the business has the capability to take on new projects
- ensuring that resources are working to drive the business's strategic goals
- managing the planning horizon and modelling multiple resource scenarios
- identifying operational resource bottlenecks

Within all organisations, resource demands will usually exceed supply and there are always too many projects and not enough resources to carry them out well. However, many project selection methods and processes do a poor job of resource balancing because they do not understand the business's capability to take on new projects. Many organisations simply consider individual projects one at a time and on their own merits, with little regard for the impact that one project has on the next. Worse yet, people resources are assigned to projects, but only later is it discovered that the same people are committed to multiple projects, and that those same people are overallocated. In essence projects are evaluated with no strategic view in mind, 'go' decisions are made and resource implications are often not factored in. This cascades down the pipeline. Gridlock ends up plaguing many project portfolio processes simply because they lack visibility of and control over their resources.

For a PPM process to be successful, the organisation needs this visibility of and control over resources in order to ensure that it has the right people on the right jobs at the right time. Effective PPM is about the ability to view resource allocation across all projects, programmes and the portfolio and also have the ability to reallocate these resources to more critical activities and to factor this into any forward planning.

In order to better understand your business's capability, three key components need to be factored into organising for PPM:

- *A single integrated resource and skills database*: It is essential that the PPM implementation is designed to handle automatic resource allocation, facilitated by an underlying skills database drawn from a single data source.
- *'What if' scenario analysis capability*: Advanced scenario modelling provides the 'what-if' capabilities to examine multiple scenarios so as to help fine-tune assumptions about projected resource usage, performance and milestones, and is essential to planning and forecasting the future direction of the project portfolio. This allows resource plans to be tested for feasibility, matching against skills, competencies, experience and availability. 'What if' scenarios give the portfolio process the ability to match supply and demand and clearly demonstrate to the rest of the business where potential shortfalls exist.
- *Dashboard visibility of resources*: PPM needs to deliver dynamic visibility by aligning resources with organisational capacities. Dashboard visibility, as outlined earlier, enables the business to drill down and drill up though capability management data by allowing all relevant roles and layers of management to efficiently measure and monitor in real time the business's internal and external resources demands. Dashboard visibility allows you to receive automatic notifications on work slippage, capacity issues, and other concerns while extending

your planning horizon, allowing the business to engage in capacity planning months in advance.

3.10   Establishing a project management maturity baseline for PPM

The level of project management maturity within the business is critical to the deployment of PPM. It was stated earlier that it is simply not enough for the business to manage the project portfolio mix without the management of the projects themselves. The success of PPM fundamentally comes down to project management proficiency, in other words, how well or how badly the business currently manages the project process. Greater project management maturity is presumed to indicate greater capability for successfully selecting, authorising, planning, executing, controlling and closing out projects and programmes that achieve the strategic goals of the organisation.

When assessing project management maturity the business will learn how projects are typically managed and what processes and tools usually exist at each of five maturity levels. The business will also learn how to assess either a department's or the whole organisation's maturity level, identify obstacles that prevent attainment of high maturity levels, and indicate how executives can promote project management.

The project management maturity model is typically described as follows, and as shown in Figure 16:

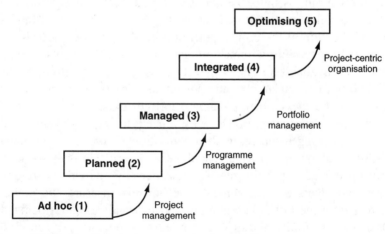

Figure 16 Levels of project management maturity

- *Level 1, Ad hoc*: Inconsistent project management skills and processes are applied in an ad hoc fashion across the organisation. Teams are functionally isolated.
- *Level 2, Planned*: Individual, single projects are planned effectively. Processes are in place to track scope, schedule and cost, and to repeat earlier successes on projects with similar applications. There is a growing awareness by the organisation that projects are part of overall programmes that must also be planned.
- *Level 3, Managed*: Integrated, cross-functional programme teams are the norm within the organisation. Consistent planning processes are defined, documented and used by all projects within a programme. Individual project plans are integrated into overall programme plans.
- *Level 4, Integrated*: Standard programme and project management processes are documented, supported and used across the organisation. A portfolio management process is also documented, supported and used. Systematic tracking of projects and programmes is carried out across the organisation. The infrastructure needed to collect portfolio management data is in place. Detailed measures of the project management process are collected. A project cost accounting system is in place.
- *Level 5, Optimised*: Fluid, independent teams plan and manage projects cross-functionally. Decisions are driven proactively through up-to-date project information.

The discipline of project management has focused on how to successfully complete projects, deliver project content, satisfy project stakeholders, and manage schedules, resources, costs, deadlines and quality. While project management achieves *project success*, PPM is the natural progression and is designed to achieve *business success*.

Project Management Maturity Assessment (PMMA) is both a reference model for appraising an organisation's project management process maturity, as well as a process model for helping organisations develop disciplined, predictable project management processes. Once a PMMA baseline has been established, the model provides specific guidance for moving to the next level and is critical to (1) understanding the business's readiness for PPM; (2) achieving organisational and domain level involvement of the PPM implementation; (3) providing a method for continual assessment of the level of project competency as PPM is embedded within the organisation. Therefore conducting a PMMA will enable the business to gauge the level of maturity, enabling the organisation to tackle the barriers to adoption set out in the following subsections.

3.10.1 Quality of project environment

Poor strategic vision prevents the organisation attaching a strategic ROI to project delivery. Moreover, a poor project environment hinders best practice project governance and reduces the quality of standardised project management techniques throughout the organisation. Therefore typical areas that need to be assessed are the processes for ensuring:

- strategic orientation
- management of the multi-project environment
- organisational support for project management
- fostering of attitudes towards project management
- quality of project team relations
- quality of meetings

3.10.2 How projects are initiated

A poor project initiation process prevents the business from achieving a consensus among key stakeholders and project personnel on the scope and schedule of a project and the effort required for project success, which radically reduces the chances of successful execution. This prevents the business from gaining consensus on project expectations, proactively defining and managing initial project risks, and identifying and managing dependencies between multiple projects. Therefore typical areas that need to be assessed are the processes for:

- proposing projects
- scoping projects
- approving projects
- establishing project teams
- assigning roles and responsibilities
- defining project parameters and planning strategy
- establishing the project framework

3.10.3 How projects are planned and executed

The two biggest barriers to successful project management are poor project planning and the organisation's inability to develop a project execution that is repeatable, institutional and successful. Businesses suffer from fragmented methodologies in which planning and execution are attributable to the individual project manager rather than to the business.

Organisations are unable to drive accountability, fine-tune processes and assess the impact on the business. Therefore typical areas that need to be assessed are the processes for:

- use of standard planning tools and procedures
- preparing preliminary schedules and work breakdown structure
- developing a preliminary integrated schedule
- refining estimates
- resource management
- reviewing plan quality
- optimisation
- risk assessment and management
- transition to management
- establishing the baseline plan
- revalidating business cases for projects
- agreement and approval of project plans
- communication of project 'go-live' to project stakeholders
- agreeing a timeframe for next project review

3.10.4 How project progress is reported, communicated and tracked

Poor project visibility and reporting granularity have a major impact on the ability of the business to deliver successful projects. Typical problems range from the inability to track only top-priority project investments, to track all projects at a high level, and to track project-specific details such as milestones, resources utilisation, deliverables, assignments and tasks. Businesses are in effect unable to identify and address exceptions and risks when they are actionable. Therefore typical areas that need to be assessed are the processes for:

- collecting project data
- reporting project status
- ensuring quality and accuracy of reporting
- carrying out variance analysis and adaptive action

3.10.5 How projects are closed

Many businesses simply do not have the processes nor infrastructure in place to ensure that all project deliverables are completed, that all project documentation is catalogued and filed, and that there is consensus between key stakeholders and project personnel that the project is complete. The business in effect *relies on the individual manager or the discretion of the project team* to close projects, without any feedback on lessons learned and on how the business can ensure the successful delivery of future projects. Therefore typical areas that need to be assessed are the processes for:

- closing a project
- documenting lessons learned
- understanding a project's impact on the business strategy

CHAPTER 4

Select the PPM tool-set

4.1 Project-centric applications vs the PPM solution

Organising the business's people, and organising its processes, are the most important components in deploying PPM successfully. The software tools used in PPM primarily represent a way to automate the processes, to make them more effective and efficient by reducing human error and tedious administration to a minimum. It is vital to understand that simply possessing a PPM software tool does not mean that you have a PPM process and are actively managing your projects as a portfolio of investments. Simply put, avoid 'pure play' software vendors who are unable to provide a detailed PPM process package. Instead manage tool-set selection as part of comprehensive consultation led programme that focuses on delivering the organisation of people, processes and software as part of an integrated package.

There are many software tools in the marketplace that can assist the business in implementing portfolio management. Some tools are specifically targeted at the portfolio management space, while other tools are complementary and assist in various specific areas such as programme and project management.

At a minimum, software packages should include the following:

- portfolio allocation, tracking and management
- workload allocation, management and forecasting
- project based timesheet capture and reporting
- project management and programme management scheduling tools
- resource management, scheduling and allocation
- demand management, including documenting needs, prioritisation, skills requirements, time and cost estimating and approval
- financial and budget reporting
- dashboard tools, including portfolio, programme and resource visibility

Even though people and process implementation will usually take precedence, in some instances tool-set selection may also require that specific processes be followed. Whatever the case, the skill is in balancing the three components and ensuring that correct tool selection aids efficient process implementation and vice versa. As will be outlined in Chapter 6 (section 6.8), the PoB allows the organisation to synergise, through trial and error, tool selection with 'people and process build' in a low risk environment without adversely impacting business-as-usual activities or incurring the political fallout and cost of a problematic software implementation.

In this chapter we will examine some of the key technical issues involved when selecting a PPM tool, then turn our attention to understanding in detail a PPM tool-set's key features and capabilities. Three critical considerations will be addressed:

- Firstly, we will explore some of the drawbacks with implementing a purely project-centric tool-set, and we then examine how project portfolio management fundamentally differs in this regard.
- Secondly, we will provide a list of best practice considerations or *essential solution USPs* (unique selling points) to ensure that the PPM tool-set is able to exert leverage on and integrate into other parts of the business.
- Finally, we will explore and profile the core features and capabilities of a PPM tool-set. We will pay particular attention to the following elements, which make up the core components of such a tool-set:
  o portfolio management
  o resource management
  o programme management
  o project management
  o timesheet management
  o budget and financial management
  o role based dashboards

When selecting a PPM tool it is essential to be wary of purely project-centric tools that focus only on the project delivery process. This is not to suggest that project-level data (phases, deliverables, schedule, budget, and so on) is not an absolutely essential component for effective portfolio management – it is paramount and forms the baseline information for successful portfolio management. However, a PPM tool is above all a business tool, not a project management tool. Therefore, in addition to interfacing with a project management environment, that is, tasks, activities, schedules and so on, a PPM tool should support a business interpretation of the project management process and should look to empower executives with information relevant to their position within the organisation. For example, some of the key business components of a PPM tool should include:

- role based dashboard environment
- portfolio management
- programme and project management
- resource management and capability analysis
- project governance and milestone management
- 'what if' scenario analysis
- budget and financial project management reporting

What are the drawbacks of using a purely project-centric tool? The focus on project-centric tools will result in a struggle to operate effectively in an organisation where:

- there are many projects in operation at any one time
- different areas in the business are competing for a limited set of resources
- the availability of resources or given skills can severely affect the progress of the project
- project timescales vary because of the complexity of their nature
- clients' requirements are regularly changing

Many organisations tend to focus on individual project choices, made one at a time with little regard for the impact that one project has on the next. Moreover, project-centric tools typically have the reputation of being in the domain of the project manager, not that of the business, divorced from the executive decision making stream. The result is poor quality project information and an imbalanced portfolio which leads to *project-by-project decision making.* In other words, the business suffers from too many projects that have a bias toward the short term, which are relatively low in value and carry minimal risk. When riskier projects are put onto the agenda, management does not have the necessary visibility of the business's capability and is not prepared to initiate the project. Most importantly, many project-centric tools are unable to roll milestones up and down the organisation in order to give a business view of what is and what is not being delivered.

However, there remains within businesses a tremendous gap between the perceived applications and the practical realities of what is needed to implement a true PPM system. Even though businesses are showing increasing interest in knowing where the organisation's resources are committed and what ROI the organisation is getting from its project investments, many of them have traditionally been weak in selecting tools for managing projects within an enterprise business environment. Businesses have tended to focus on single-user project-centric applications with little or no regard to how these do or do not impact the business.

How does a PPM tool differ? Traditional project management systems are capable of recording plans, results and reporting project performance against schedules and budget targets. A fully featured PPM tool looks to organising data from multiple projects to coincide with specified strategic criteria. Whereas project planning tools focus on the operational aspects of project delivery, a PPM tool should provide for continual strategic assessment and optimisation, enabling the business to undertake the following iterative steps:

- align projects with business strategy
- make project selection and prioritisation decisions
- manage and balance the project portfolio pipeline
- analyse resource demand and capability
- track project portfolio performance
- initiate corrective project portfolio action

4.2 Essential solution unique selling points (USPs)

A key determinant of the successful implementation of a PPM solution is the selection of the right tool-set and how it integrates with the rest of the business. Selecting the right tool-set can make or break the implementation of a PPM process. Moreover, ensuring people know what is going to be involved, and are fully supportive of the effort to purchase and implement software, is critical. It is also essential for the business to understand that:

- The tool is there to support the 'people and process' side of the PPM deployment. Simply having PPM software on your desktop does not mean you are doing PPM.
- PPM tool-set selection involves a complex process of business modelling, software analysis, evaluation and buying, not simply installing a shrink-wrapped, ready-to-run piece of software.
- Selection will require a rigorous process involving a number of people over a number of weeks or months.
- The evaluation process is an investment and the business will need an 'evaluation budget'.

- The evaluation process will bring the need for a PoB, for which both physical and human resources will have to made available.
- The evaluation process will not only need to involve experienced technical people but will also require senior sponsorship as it needs to approached from a business perspective not a pure IT perspective.
- The organisation will need to be prepared to consider the changes within key business processes and to ensure that the right environment is modelled within the evaluation process.

Before we get into the PPM tool-set's features, it is essential that when selecting a PPM tool-set the following key issues are factored into your planning:

- *Out-of-the-box vs integrated solutions*: There are essentially two types of PPM solution: integrated, and best-of-breed out-of-the-box solutions. The former have typically emerged from the ERP space and provide for complete integration with back-office functions such as finance, HR, procurement, and so on. These are essentially large and very costly 'rip-and-replace' applications that do not have the flexibility of the smaller and more agile alternatives. The out-of-the box solutions, sometimes known as 'pure play specialist' applications, focus their core functionality solely around PPM. They are typically much lighter and are geared towards quick deployment and affordability. In addition, 'pure play specialist' applications will typically provide all the benefits of strong integration capabilities with systems such as those for accounting, HR, payroll, and CRM, thus easily adapting to an organisation's current IT infrastructure.
- *Avoid 'rip and replace'*: A 'rip and replace' scenario strains the company's culture and human capital – employees are in effect forced to abandon what they know about current system operations and learn a whole new set of applications. The cost of learning new tools, and the adverse impact of this on productivity – a factor often not considered by management when implementing a new system – can be very high.
- *Web based solutions*: Collaboration and communication are critical to successful portfolio management, so the tool-set should be web enabled, and provide an intuitive interface. Web based applications will significantly reduce the hardware and implementation overheads traditionally associated with the client footprint, that is, where software is installed locally on the user's PC. Web based applications enable the business to rapidly facilitate upgrades and customisation, with no physical impact on the individual user's environment.

- *Web publishing*: The tool-set needs to come with variety of means for disseminating project data and reports via the Web, including support for XML, MS Word, MS Excel, CSV, HTML and PDF formats.

- *Data conversion issues*: When choosing software, users often assume that they can get their data moved from their old system to the new system without much of a problem. The fact is that data conversion is often the single biggest headache when putting in a new system. Be sure to get a specific proposal on exactly what data is going to be moved and check it carefully after it is moved.

- *Third-party integration and ODBC compliance*: It is essential to be able to post and interrogate project data in an open, SQL-type database format – traditionally called ODBC. ODBC compliance provides for easy data manipulation and extraction and allows the PPM solution to be integrated with corporate systems such as ERP, accounting packages, MS Project and MS Office. Common third-party applications include:
  - o Oracle Financials
  - o SAP
  - o Oracle and MS SQL Database
  - o Native integration with MS Project Professional
  - o MS Office, including Access and Excel
  - o Crystal Decisions
  - o Support for XML, CSV, and fixed data exchange

- *Reporting capability*: When project and operations data is integrated it often become voluminous. In order to interrogate the data and reduce it to meaningful information, it is essential to look for solutions that are able to integrate with OLAP based 'slice and dice' analysis engines.

- *Interface ease of use*: The system should allow easy access by a wide variety of personnel, from dispersed locations, via networked and web based protocols. The design of the various screens must facilitate ease of comprehension by a wide range of individuals, using popular icon metaphors and graphics.

- *Self-contained*: The tool-set should be self-contained, to enable centrally managed implementation and control of life cycles, security settings and entitlements (hierarchical, role based), business cases, status reports, stage-gate reviews and approvals, and analytics for resource, schedule and budget management. A self-contained tool will help reduce maintenance complexity and ensure that all the analytics required to support portfolio management are sourced from a central database.

- *Configurability vs customisation*: It is obvious that one size does not fit all. A flexible, out-of-the-box, easily configured and modifiable application has distinct advantages. Since business conditions change frequently, the ideal application will not require significant customisation or ongoing vendor support such as recoding of the software, even when major changes or new (ad hoc) reports are desired. Remember that changes to software code mean expense additional to that of the initial deployment, and upgrades may be more difficult to accomplish.
- *Hierarchical capability*: The tool-set should be easily configured with hierarchical, role based security and entitlements to support the diverse groups and organisations providing data to the system.
- *Security features*: The tool-set should provide for excellent security capability to protect the confidentiality of the project portfolio – particularly financial information. This should include the following types of features:
  - password based login
  - exclusive, shared and read-only modes for data access
  - user-, group- and role-level security
  - selective read/write permissions by user or group
  - group-level settings and controls
  - role-level settings to control functionality within a data object such as a project or resource file
  - SSL encryption between client and server
- *Role based training provision*: It is essential that the PPM tool-set come with a flexible training programme in the form of demonstrations, discussions, online interactivity and hands-on exercises. There should be a wide range of role based training programmes designed to address relevant business and technical positions, which should typically include:
  - *End user*: This type of package should be aimed at general staff usage and designed to provide users with the necessary familiarisation skills to get up and running as quickly as possible. Training needs to be tailored for lower usage by providing users with a basic introduction and guide on how the individual modular components function.
  - *Management*: This type of package needs to be focused on providing key project stakeholders with the technical and business skills necessary to successfully set up, manage and administer the system. This training focuses on delving deeper into the system's core capabilities and should be designed to enable managers to control things like resourcing, budgeting, project planning, and

configuring role based views, as well as linking to third-party project management applications.

- o *Technical/systems administration*: This type of package should provide designated technical and systems administrators with a comprehensive training programme that includes all user aspects as outlined above, plus the technical training required to support the implementation and to maintain the system.
- o *Training the trainer*: For businesses with high numbers of users and a restricted budget, 'training the trainer' packages will enable a designated individual to be trained to a satisfactory level for training future users.
- o *Bespoke training*: It is essential that training programmes be fully configured to the needs of the business.

4.3 Software as a Service (SaaS) / Application Service Providers (ASPs)

We stated earlier that it was crucial for businesses deploying a PPM process and tool-set to look at replacing their desktop application with a collaborative web based environment. We now extend this discussion and look at Application Service Providers (ASPs) or what is commonly termed Software as a Service (SaaS), delivering PPM tools as a low cost infrastructure and low risk deployment option.

The SaaS model levers the developments in Web 2.0 to deliver the same features and functions as desktop programmes, including rich user interfaces and fast feedback via a web-only infrastructure. The current jostling and market competition between the software giants Google and Microsoft is very typical of developments within the SaaS space. Both Google and Microsoft are pioneering the latest developments (Google Office and Microsoft Office Live) to migrate into online, web based environments with the next generation of more dynamic, business-responsive applications. Compared with the desktop environment, the SaaS model provides many compelling benefits, the most significant being the ability to have truly 'stateless' computing. In other words, wherever the user goes their data goes with them. This means there is no need to synchronise data, and the application runs on practically any computer, as long as the operating system supports a standard web browser.

According to IT analysts Gartner, SaaS applications present a cost-effective alternative to in-house software licensing options – especially for small to medium sized enterprises. As we will outline below, SaaS allows small companies to get 'good enough' enterprise application functionality such as a PPM tool, in a model that works for them, leaving the IT skills and capital investment burdens to the service provider. SaaS offerings allow an organisation to spend more of its software investment money in critical areas, such as services, process definition, and support, as opposed to spending the bulk of the investment money merely on implementing technology. SaaS allows an organisation to focus on automating proven processes in shorter periods of time (compared to in-house deployments), without committing to a long term (multi-year, multi-phased implementation) relationship with one vendor.

SaaS as a network of web based business services is now becoming widely used within the PPM market as a quick, low cost, low risk method of deploying software across the enterprise. In its simplest form SaaS manages and distributes services and solutions to customers across a secure internet connection or a private network from a remote, central data centre. The core feature of SaaS is that users do not need to purchase, install and maintain the software themselves; instead they rent the applications they need from their SaaS provider as part of a consultation driven PPM initiative. SaaS providers offer companies services that would otherwise have to be provided in-house, or on-site. The need for SaaS has evolved from the increasing costs of specialised software, which have far exceeded the price range of small to medium sized businesses. Also, the growing complexities of software have led to huge costs in distributing the software to end users. In essence, through SaaS, the complexities and costs of such software can be cut down.

The key advantages of using this model are that:

- It provides a low cost of entry to build a business case and gain executive-level buy-in.
- It allows the business to build a PPM process and embed competency without being bogged down in protracted software installation cycles.
- It allows the business to work around IT resource and budget constraints.
- The vendor's application can be tested in a proof-of-concept or pilot.
- The SaaS provider owns, operates and maintains the software application.
- The SaaS provider owns, operates and maintains the servers that run the application.
- The SaaS provider employs the people needed to maintain the application.

- The SaaS provider responds on demand to make the application available to additional users within the business either via a browser or through some sort of 'thin client'.
- The SaaS provider bills for the application either on a per-user basis or on a monthly/annual fee basis.
- Especially for small businesses and start-ups, the biggest advantage is low cost of entry and, in most cases, an extremely short setup time.
- The SaaS model, as with any outsourcing arrangement, reduces the in-house IT headcount.
- The SaaS model also eliminates specialised IT infrastructure for the application as well as for supporting applications.
- The SaaS model can shift internet bandwidth to the provider, who can often provide it at lower cost.

However, plan cautiously if any of the following situations exist:

- Heavy IT involvement is required to support business process and data integration:
  - Integration into other applications not being hosted, such as campaign management, lead management, event management and sales force automation, is complex.
  - Integration into other business applications, such as ERP, supply chain and finance, is also complex.
- Data support and security issues:
  - Where depth of functionality is required. Not all SaaS applications offer deep functionality. Those that do tend to be more expensive. Cheaper, subscription based applications have lighter functional capabilities.
  - Where flexibility and configurability are highly valued. Not all SaaS applications offer great flexibility and configurability. Again, those that do tend to cost more.

For a PPM deployment, SaaS provides a low cost, low risk environment, for these reasons:

- Firstly, during the proof-of-benefit (PoB) stage (see Chapter 6), SaaS ensures that you do not incur unnecessary software trialling costs. For example, many organisations have to spend their dedicated evaluation budgets buying or renting hardware servers in order to install the software and to create a model environment.

- Secondly, following a successful PoB, the impact of a rollout is kept to a minimum since the application is simply pushed out via a thin client on the user's desktop.
- Thirdly, there is the growing complexity of software and software upgrades. Distributing huge, complex applications to the end user has become extremely expensive from a customer service standpoint, and upgrades further down the road make the problem worse.
- Fourthly, SaaS also delivers a platform for seamless integration into line-of-business applications, which means greater long term flexibility, allowing applications to grow and change over time as business requirements evolve. In the desktop software model, vendors sell end-user licenses and also sell costly software based consultancy services that focus on heavy customisation and one-off integrations. The typical problem that businesses suffer from with regard to this approach is that the vendor walks away when the engagement is over, and doesn't reappear until the next upgrade cycle comes along.

The key questions to ask when choosing an SaaS model are:

- Who owns the data?
- What are the levels of support?
- How do users access the software application?
- How are service issues resolved?
- How are questions and/or problems concerning the software resolved, and what happens next?
- Is training provided?
- How secure is the data?
- What are your internal security policies in respect of allowing SaaS employees to have passwords and access to reports?
- What are the security safeguards against external attack, and do you provide backups to handle hardware failures?
- How secure is the connection between the infrastructure and the user? Is it secured by encryption, a VPN, proprietary techniques or some other system?
- How is the application served, is the data on a dedicated machine or a shared machine?
- How does the SaaS provider handle redundancy? What levels of redundancy are in place to keep your servers online?
- How does the SaaS provider handle hardware/software problems?
- How does the SaaS provider handle a disaster such as fire or flood?

- How would the SaaS provider handle the complete loss of the facility? How long would it be before they restored service?
- How can you get the data out if you choose to select a new SaaS provider?

4.4   Software deployment considerations

In Chapter 6 we will explore in detail how to kick-start the PPM process and we will examine the PoB model as a low risk deployment method. However, when selecting a software tool-set we recommend that the following additional key factors be taken into consideration:

- *Technical groundwork*: Make an assessment of your existing technical environment (systems, processes, and so on) before deploying any PPM software tool. The assessment is designed to aid the vendor understand the client needs in detail. It is at this stage that you will learn where you are and where you can go.
- *Collaborative deployment planning*: It is essential that you work with the vendor in developing a roadmap that outlines timeframe, deployment activities, deliverables, milestones training and resources.
- *Role based user model*: The vendor team should work with you to define how each identified role in your organisation (executive, PM, programmer, and so on) should use the tool. It is essential that you work closely to design the processes and metrics in order to create a role based user model.
- *Pilot installation and configuration*: The vendor should install the PPM tool-set within a pilot environment. It is essential that you interact with the pilot version of the configured tool-set to ensure that needs are met. This is when adjustments should be made, before a full deployment takes place.
- *Rollout*: This should be phased and seamless and should not negatively impact business-as-usual activities. The vendor should supply all technical documentation and training materials during rollout.
- *Tool administration*: The vendor should work closely with your system administrator and database administrator to define a roadmap for tools administration and maintenance procedures, roles and responsibilities.
- *Follow-up*: The vendor should follow up with your end users to get feedback on performance. This is also an opportunity to have questions asked and answered that were not raised before.

4.5 Solution features and capabilities

We have identified the fact that a PPM tool-set needs to support the 'people and process' rollout by being able to address the following key issues:

- aligning your projects with the business's strategic goals
- identifying, qualifying, selecting, prioritising and funding projects that address the business strategy
- measuring performance to ensure that projects are collectively meeting the portfolio strategy
- managing organisational resource demand, capacity, and capability to ensure that the right people are on the right projects
- identifying and taking corrective actions on projects/programmes not in compliance with portfolio objectives and commitments
- establishing effective communication and reporting mechanisms that enable timely, fact based decision making regarding projects, programmes, and the overall portfolio.

Undoubtedly the flavour of the project portfolio management process will largely depend on the kinds of projects involved; the source of the projects, whether they be specifically for the benefit of external clients or designed to support the internal operations of the business; and the type of business driving the projects. Whatever the makeup of your business's project landscape, a PPM solution will need to comprise the following core features, functionality and capabilities as a minimum.

4.5.1 Portfolio management

The portfolio functionality needs to provide the business with a structured approach to evaluating, selecting, and prioritising projects. It needs to align projects with the corporate strategy and provide the necessary information to allow the business to invest in the right projects at the right time. To help with deciding which projects to start, end or put on hold and also where to allocate resources, budgets and time, the portfolio analysis functionality should have a number of features, including:

- *Hierarchical drill-down and drill-up capability*: The PPM solution needs to provide high-level drill-down and drill-up capability to view the entire project portfolio. An essential component of the portfolio management feature is the ability for projects to be rolled into programmes and to be grouped by business unit, division and department, providing a powerful cross-enterprise view of project status.

- *Governance, strategy alignment and milestone tracking*: The purpose of a project is to advance one or more business objectives. Most projects start out closely aligned with these objectives, but gaps inevitably appear. We have discussed earlier the fact that by elevating the prioritisation and oversight responsibilities to the executive level (embedded within the PPM process), project portfolio management ensures that projects receive the backing they need to succeed. Executives have the authority and business knowledge to ensure alignment between projects and business strategies; to fine-tune the timing and order of projects to exploit synergies, avoid re-works and eliminate redundancies; to optimally assign resources; to direct funds to the most valuable initiatives; and to help resolve critical performance issues. The PPM tool-set needs to be able to view and assess information that accurately reflects the critical 'milestones' that affect business performance and to see whether projects are currently aligned with the business's objectives and goals. Therefore an essential component of PPM is the ability of the business to view critical milestones at any preconfigured level within the organisation, not just at the traditional task based level typical of many project-centric tools. Not only does milestone tracking help to embed project governance into the PPM process; it is also designed to provide the business with the ability to evaluate and track the list of projects against current strategic objectives. At a minimum, milestones need to be tracked at the following levels:
  - Portfolio
  - Programme
  - Project
  - Work packages

and/or
  - Company
  - Group
  - Department
  - Team

The status of these milestones needs to be real-time, and they need to give the business instant visibility of answers to these questions:
  - Are they on time?
  - Have they been moved?
  - Who moved them?
  - Why were they moved?
  - What is the impact?

- *Portfolio inventory/registry and ideas management*: The tool-set needs to have the capability to build a centralised repository to capture all project portfolio information and new ideas being fed into the portfolio pipeline. The inventory and ideas management capability provides the business case, definition, scope, risk, expected ROI, milestones, status, budget variance, and completion timeline for each project, whether it is newly proposed, that is, a fresh idea, or whether it is an active, live project. This centralised repository needs to allow the PPMT to consolidate the contents of each project into various portfolios, providing a single location for portfolio managers or executives to quickly locate important information about the portfolio.

- *Portfolio, selection, prioritisation and evaluation*: Understanding the success and performance of different projects demands the ability to measure equally the different key performance indicators and weight them appropriately to give a unified view of each project in relation to others. Therefore the PPM tool-set needs to support the capability for the PPMT to view consolidated information about projects, resources and costs for project 'go/kill/hold/fix' decisions. Measurement of capital expenses, and reviewing them against strategic goals, is an essential criterion. The functionality needs to provide for comparative views such as net present value, earned value analysis, balanced score carding, cost/benefit analysis, and so on, to aid the project prioritisation and selection process. For example, score cards which provide critical information about the health of a project, by showing overall financial and resource status, may include colour codes and arrows, such as RAG (Red, Amber, Green). This functionality can include dashboards, traffic lighting and project health assessments based on user defined metrics.

- *Capability analysis*: Fundamental to PPM is the ability to measure the planned allocation of resources according to some strategic plan. To do this, the PPM tool-set must be able to estimate the effort demanded and supplied for each project in the portfolio, and then roll up the results for strategic evaluation. Effective resource allocation typically requires an understanding of existing work or funding resource commitments (in either business operations or other projects) as well as of the skills available in the resource pool. Project investment should only be made in projects where the necessary resources are available during a specified period of time. If a project is either performing below expectations (cost overruns, benefit erosion) or is no longer aligned to business objectives (which change with natural market and statutory evolution), the functionality must enable management to choose to decommit from a project, to restrict further investment, and/or to redirect resources towards other projects that better fit business objectives.

- *'What if' scenario modelling*: Advanced modelling should provide the 'what if' capability to examine multiple scenarios to help fine-tune assumptions about projected resource usage, performance and milestones. The ability to produce multiple profiles for different scenarios removes any guesswork and wishful thinking from the budgeting, planning and resourcing processes (see Figure 17). Scenario modelling provides the ability to take a live plan offline, adjust it to reflect new business priorities, and review the impact across the whole organisation. If acceptable, it can be used to replace the live plan or be stored for future reference as a full record of your modelling activity. As a result, the organisation can quickly react to changes in strategic direction, new competition entering the market or, more importantly, it can see the effect of such 'change' as part of a global corporate perspective.

4.5.2   Resource management

Ensuring that resource allocation always reflects an organisation's overall business capability is a fundamental underpinning of PPM. For maximum efficiency, resource managers need to be able to create and share resource

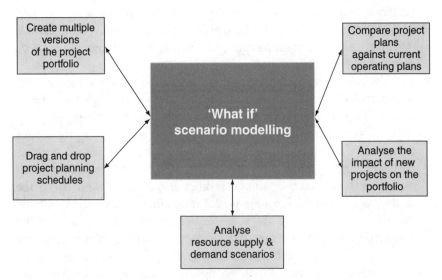

Figure 17 Key capabilities of 'what if' scenario planning

breakdown structures across the enterprise and dynamically allocate resources according to availability of skills.

Resource management should enable the business to:

- locate and deploy available best-fit resources
- reduce underallocated resource time, match available resources to projects, keep the resource-idle time down, and minimise resources that are on the bench
- view resource use in real time and identify resources with open time-frames of availability, with or without reliance on creating a project
- identify potential shortfalls and act before they occur
- compare project demand to resource use and capacity and take action on it via recruitment, workforce procurement, outsourcing or rejection/approval of a project request
- achieve an equitable balance between resource demand and supply
- query resource levels across the entire organisation
- identify and track key skills and experience

Resource management features within a PPM tool-set may be at various levels. These range from ones which enable an understanding of the business's complete capability (resources, skills, geographic location, and so on) down to ones which focus on managing the skills, activities and time of an individual.

The features of the PPM tool-set should therefore cover the following resource management capabilities:

- *Capability planning*: The tool-set should provide a complete understanding of all resources across the business and how they can be aligned to meet strategic objectives and programme/project needs.
- *Resource supply (capability) and demand management*: As a project is built, the tool-set needs to be able to plan and manage resource supply and balance this against work demand. Via dashboard capability, managers should have the ability to query resource supply and demand across the entire organisational structure, rolling up and drilling down to the different hierarchical levels. It is essential that resources can be intelligently supplied through skills search and dynamic allocation. The functionality needs to enable understanding of the skill-sets of individuals and track their development, experience and interests. Also, the tool-set has to give managers the ability to see resources or skills shortfalls due to project overlap or slippage.
- *Resource scheduling*: Once the demand has been supplied and a project is under way, the system should allow for the scheduling of available

resources through a scheduling tool. This should allow for quick and easy resource allocation which can be monitored and adjusted as projects are undertaken.

- *Team management*: The ability to manage resources across projects and programmes needs to be supplemented with the ability to manage resources at team and department levels. Knowing where your people are, what they are working on and where they will be going helps keep track of your team and your internal capability. Secondment of resources, skills, training, growth and recruitment can all be tracked at a team level.

- *Resource management profile*: Individual staff members are a complex and hard to manage resource in themselves, with many aspects that need regular attention. The workload needed to manage each person can be a significant cost on the business. Reducing administration through timesheet management, expense management, personal information management and skills/training management through an intuitive and centralised system can massively reduce administration costs as well as improve the level of management. Timesheet and expense approval, skills and training management as well as personal details are all available through a single resource dashboard.

4.5.3 Programme management

The programme management capability needs to be designed to support the PMO and to provide it with valuable intelligence about all projects in the organisation: ongoing projects, proposed new projects, and those that are on hold. Its core functionality should at a minimum focus on the following:

- managing change requests
- receiving requests for work and resources
- controlling resource allocation and utilisation
- tracking project execution as well as issues and risks
- allowing the PMO personnel to consolidate information from multiple projects
- providing the PMO with real-time status indicators and reports on all projects
- enabling document management, approval workflow and version control
- enabling the PMO to plan globally, and schedule and report across the enterprise

- providing centralised security and administration, making it easy to coordinate and automate global project changes
- providing capacity planning analysis to enable the PMO to see gaps and surpluses in the workforce
- providing template management to enable the PMO to create, control and monitor templates to facilitate governance and adherence to project control standards
- enabling issue management so that the PMO can provide a standardised approach to documenting, assessing, resolving and escalating issues and risks
- providing opportunity management to enable the PMO to understand what new business is forthcoming and to plan for the work ahead of time
- providing resource management to enable the PMO to control resource allocation and utilisation
- providing financial management to enable the PMO to easily track both project revenue and project costs
- providing document management and approvals to ensure that everyone is up to date with the most current information in accordance with security settings
- providing resource planning views to help programme managers find the best available resources

4.5.4 Project management

The PPM tool-set should either come with inbuilt project management capability and/or enable native integration with traditional task based applications like MS Project. The project management component of PPM should provide for a centralised, integrated repository of all project related work and activity. This repository should be visible via role based dashboards to the relevant project managers. The primary goal of the tool-set should be that of enabling the business to manage and deliver on the full project life cycle.

Key capabilities and features should at a minimum include those relating to:

- *project life cycle*: creating processes to manage the entire life cycle of a project, with support for:
    - o large, multi-phased projects and programmes
    - o multiple project processes or methodologies

- o creation of project-specific phases, with project status trackable by phase
- o creation of optional, project defined phase reviews (or gate reviews)
- o management of deliverables, milestones, activities, work packages and/or tasks
- o creation of deliverables checklists
- o deliverables sign-off
- o linking deliverables to documents and/or other information that ensures delivery
- o saving project life cycle processes to templates and applying them to new projects
- *project scheduling*: enabling project managers to collaborate with team members on essential project deliverables, with work groups able to share and collaborate on essential tasks and associated milestones such as:
  - o assigning, viewing and monitoring tasks across the project team
  - o viewing task assignments in each personal workspace, and easily updating tasks completed
  - o updating task status in real time
  - o view real-time reports such as those on late tasks, tasks falling due, resource allocation and overallocation
  - o creating task reports by resource
  - o enabling email alerts when new tasks are assigned
  - o create links between tasks and other objects such as issues, decisions, change requests, documents, and so on
  - o building project action items, issues, decisions, and so on
- *project planning*: creating a consistent method of planning and distributing project plans using a centralised web portal, with support for:
  - o storing all project data in a central data repository
  - o dashboard access to enable employees, project managers and executives to quickly and efficiently access project planning information
  - o standardisation of project planning and resource allocation
  - o Gantt views to schedule tasks, create dependencies and assign resources
  - o a two-way link to ensure project plans are updated with the latest actual information logged from timesheet and expense information
  - o providing data to track a project's progress, down to estimate-to-complete data
  - o personal calendars and to-do lists

4.5.5 Timesheet management

An essential component of PPM, as of any project planning process, is the ability of the business to provide an accurate and reliable breakdown of business-as-usual activities vis-à-vis project-centric activities. Timesheet management provides the most important baseline measure within a PPM tool-set; it gives the business the ability to track time spent on both project and non-project work, then enables the business to understand the cost and time associated with these.

The timesheet management component must allow the posting of time to all projects in the system, and should support various means of remote entry. The tool-set should also provide for management review and control of time reporting and in some environments, the time entry tools must also support progressing of the work, including revised estimate-to-complete data.

Key capabilities should include those to:

- record time and expense for project tasks and activity
- route timesheets and expenses for approval
- lock timesheet approval data
- capture and report on billable and non-billable hours
- report on missing and timesheet exceptions, such as 'overdue' and 'awaiting approval'
- define timesheet periods
- provide summary and detailed timesheet reporting
- enable work to be assigned, or users to select what projects/tasks to work on
- support work policy enforcement, such as minimum and maximum work-time rules
- support electronic timesheet overtime and pay-rule policies
- track project progress by comparing budgeted, estimated, and actual work done
- multi-client invoicing/charge-back capability for time, expenses and charges
- track and report on budgets for users, projects, and tasks

Timesheet management also allows the business to gain an accurate overview of its expenditure, income and profitability as well as focusing on time and billing from a project management perspective.

Typical benefits derived from the timesheet component include those of:

- managing time billing more effectively
- increasing control over budgets, fixed bid projects and employee related time
- tracking cost and revenue rate rules
- billing expenditures
- automating project compliance with work and employee regulations
- increasing project visibility, employee productivity and operational efficiency
- monitoring time and expenses by project, preventing budget overruns
- reducing time misappropriation
- reducing payroll preparation time
- automating reporting on absenteeism and erroneous entries

4.5.6   Budget and financial management

Access to accurate, project based financial information is a mandatory feature so that the organisation can make better and faster business decisions and invest money for maximum return.

The PPM tool-set should provide the ability to:

- align spend with projects of greatest return
- utilise project based budgets to make better decisions
- manage project budgets against financial objectives
- make project budgets transparent to all project stakeholders

The functionality required in delivering the above value and benefits includes that to:

- budget billable and non-billable projects
- budget revenue and expenses
- configure budget rules
- define multi-year and rolling budgets
- define flexible rates for the budget
- establish multiple rate hierarchies
- integrate with third-party general ledger systems
- budget project cost charge-back
- compare incurred with budgeted cost charge-back
- include capital expenditures
- track incremental project funding
- log major expenditure requests
- provide real-time vs historical data views

4.5.7 Role based dashboards

In Chapter 3 we outlined the way in which role based visibility accelerates the time it takes between getting information, understanding that information and, most importantly, acting on it. It helps the organisation address its performance management needs and analyse current business conditions, trends or anomalies at a glance by ensuring that the relevant information is pushed to the relevant roles within the business.

Role based visibility is achieved via software dashboards that are designed to deliver rich and complex information direct to the desktop in a simple format relevant to each role. Dashboards are the most important and most fundamental component of a PPM solution; without a dashboard driven solution, it is virtually impossible to deliver a successful role based PPM process. Their function is to translate the systems data into something meaningful and relevant to the individual's role within the business. For example, a typical PPM system should at a minimum have the following types of configurable, out-of-the-box capabilities:

- executive management dashboard
- portfolio management dashboard
- programme management dashboard
- project management dashboard
- resource management dashboard
- team/personal dashboards

Any PPM solution should allow for the creation of unlimited dashboards for each role within your organisation. These dashboards should be personalised for the needs of the individual role within the business and should be easy to deploy, maintain and upgrade. Below we expand upon what each type of dashboard should offer.

Executive management dashboard

Executive dashboards provide an at-a-glance overview of your entire business project portfolio, including initiative status, risks, issues, key deliverables and milestones. The executive dashboard needs to be designed to give both a summary-level picture of the health of your business in a one-page snapshot, as well as drill-down capability, to view individual units, departments, programme and projects.

Key capabilities of an executive management dashboard should include the following:

- The ability to view overall project portfolio trends and forecasts. The dashboard should enable executives to undertake advanced financial modelling by linking financial profiles direct to key milestones, operational costs, revenue streams, investments and cost reductions.
- Drill-down and drill-up capability should enable executives to view programme and project details, including schedule performance, cost performance, earned value metrics, milestone dates, work breakdown structures and change control documents.
- Provision of real-time alerts identifying misaligned projects. The dashboard should enable executives to assess high-level information about portfolio, programme and project progress against the company's key performance indicators (for example, score card view, CAPEX, NPV, EVA), milestones and portfolio definition criteria, and to undertake relevant impact analysis and risk assessment (see Chapters 5 and 8).
- High-level 'what if' scenario modelling in order to understand the business's capability to deliver on work, and to redirect resources to projects and programmes that will deliver on the portfolio objectives.
- Document, inventory and gateway management capabilities that will enable executives to modify and refine business plans aligned to corporate strategy by undertaking comparison analysis throughout key stages of a programme or project.
- On-screen milestone management to enforce project governance and accountability.
- Portfolio change tracking, so that executives can easily:
  - spot changes within projects and portfolios
  - communicate with the PPMT on new project ideas
  - approve newly submitted projects
  - communicate with the PPMT on the 'go/kill/hold/fix' status of key projects.
- Action and issues management functionality, to facilitate communication with the PPMT and PMO members to enable them to share thoughts and concerns on particular programmes and project issues.

Portfolio management dashboard

When multiple projects are all working towards a single strategy, and with so many interactions and interrelationships, it can be a daunting task to understand their global effect. The key to a portfolio management dashboard is to build a complete picture of the project landscape by putting operational activity and strategy on the same page. The portfolio dashboard needs to enable the PPMT members to manage end-to-end the full portfolio management life cycle, including:

- portfolio definition, strategy alignment and ideas management
- resource and business capability analysis
- portfolio selection, prioritisation and authorisation
- portfolio execution and monitoring

Key capabilities of the portfolio management dashboard should include:

- standardised computation of NPV, ROI and other key metrics
- customisable graphics based workflow and business process management functions
- ability to roll up project and programme data into the portfolio level. The dashboard should have the capability to analyse project, programme, business unit, divisional and enterprise-level data
- ability to view portfolio information against a score card or specified valuation model based on configurable metrics including financial, schedule, resource, scope and quality control
- direct access to what-if scenario modelling and analysis of business and resource capability
- ability to assess and communicate project status, select and prioritise initiatives, resources, and assets across the project portfolio
- real-time visibility of good and bad projects for each programme and project on one screen using RAG status
- ability to identify project issues and risks, as well as gain access to other workflows and actions
- portfolio inventory information, including project scope, priorities, requirements, dependencies, and traceability
- ability to view and make project 'go/kill/hold/fix' decisions, manage and implement project course correction and change requests such as those concerning cost, resources, schedule, benefit, and so on
- ability to generate detailed or summary status reports including those on finance, resources, benefits, issues and risk, either on demand or at regular stages within the portfolio management life cycle

Programme management dashboard

The programme management dashboard is designed to display the operational status of the business's projects and help the PMO manage their interdependencies. The dashboard should enable the PMO and its team members to:

- gain real-time visibility of the status of all programme and project interdependencies

- streamline best practice project management procedures
- help manage resource schedules, costs and performance
- manage project risk and mitigation
- report upstream and downstream on all project activities to the PPMT and project managers

The programme management dashboard's capabilities should include:

- access to governance and best practice methodologies and standards to control planning practices and project management techniques such as PRINCE2
- access to document control and template management in order to enable PMO members to create, control and monitor templates to standardise project delivery processes, training, skills management and other best practice techniques and thus improve project success rates
- ability for PMO team members to build, access, update and manage a centralised inventory of project information including: project title, key personnel, project objective, dependencies, milestones, budget, portfolio priority level and stages within the life cycle
- ability to identify both individual and interdependent project risks and issues and flag against assessment of current RAG status. The dashboard should enable the PMO to drill down to assess the impact on timelines, costs and other affected projects, with access to risk mitigation documentation
- ability to create project plans, allocate resources, and define and manage budgets and key milestones
- ability for the PMO to gain visibility of day-to-day resource allocation and real-time capacity
- ability to conduct planning analysis of the business's supply and demand in order to identify staff gaps and surpluses
- two-way reporting with the PPMT so that the PMO receives all the data it needs to manage project delivery against portfolio objectives

Project management dashboard

The project management dashboard needs to provide a single view of all project information under the control of the project manager and give them the ability to push real-time reporting up within the business as well as down to team members. For example, the dashboard should provide the project manager with an instant 'one stop shop' view of milestones, issues, what is holding up a project, who can help out or where the potential risks are located. The dashboard environment needs to ensure that the project manager is able to identify problems before they escalate, and call emergencies to the business's attention before they bring about the failure of a project.

Key capabilities and features of the project management dashboard should include:

- fast dashboard loading, with optional 'hide' and 'show' buttons for non-essential data
- drill-down capability, allowing project managers to gain access to more detailed project information such as timesheets, expenses, tasks, activities, budgets, billing and other project accounting information
- ability to directly access and manage features concerning scope, planning, verification, and change management
- ability to view the effect of schedule changes on resource availability, resource allocation and costs
- 'what if' scenario modelling analysis on different versions of the project to compare costs, schedules and resource allocation
- ability to estimate budgets and negotiate scope with project budget baselines
- ability to predict project outcomes, assess project status, and identify inter-project dependencies
- colour coded RAG status warning to show when and where problems are occurring
- ability to engage in centralised, collaborative planning, meaning that less time is spent on creating project management reports from distributed data-sets
- drill-down capability to tasks in a Gantt chart and/or third-party integration with standard planning tools such as MS Project
- drill-down capability to listing of project members and their contact information and roles

Resource management dashboard

The resource management dashboard should give instant answers to the following questions about staff resource activity:

- What are the staff in question doing?
- What can they do?
- What will they be doing?
- What needs to be done?

Being able to see the capacity of the business to undertake a project is the one of the most important components of a PPM tool-set. Resource and business capability analysis equips the organisation to understand demand and supply issues and enables different type of projects within the portfolio to be given the go-ahead or not. Capacity planning and supply and demand management are central to the running of a number of complex programmes, yet so many businesses do it badly or not at all. Knowing who is available to do work, where they are needed and which projects or programmes have the greatest demand helps you gain better visibility of how your business is running day to day.

Key capabilities and features available from the dashboard should include:

- direct access to resource profiles and skill information, to enable resource managers to forecast future training, hiring, contracting and off-shoring needs
- direct access to resource scheduling, to quickly inform project managers when positions are unfilled or resources are overallocated
- direct access to scheduled completion dates for current projects in the context of new project start dates, so that staff resources can be assigned accordingly
- drill-down capability to view utilisation, in order to reduce under-allocated resource time, quickly assign staff resources to work, and achieve optimal utilisation levels
- generation of reports, to ensure that data is collected and shared with the PMO and PPMT
- direct access to resource demand and supply functionality, so resource managers can analyse supply against incoming demand
- ability to directly rebalance workloads with 'what if' scenario analysis

Team/personal dashboards

Team or personal dashboards should give users access to the operational information that is relevant to their day-to-day project and non-project work. For example, project and task activities should be easily accessible, with the ability to quickly drill down into the information for such purposes as checking expenses, adding timesheets or updating actions. At entry, these dashboards should instantly remind users of priority actions and of the need to regularly update timesheets. These dashboards should have the key benefits of:

- reducing administration costs when authorising and managing a company-wide time and expense recording system
- helping staff to organise their time more effectively and ensure business objectives are met on time

- increasing and distributing projects' visibility and accountability to the whole organisation, and enabling prevention of budget overruns and project scope creep
- reduce reporting cycles and administration workload as well as invoice time and cross-charge preparation work

Key components and features should include:

- ability to track continually changing project updates and schedules from one single integrated view
- high-level as well as drill-down capability to view latest timesheets and expenses and a profile of projects the users are currently working on that day
- ability to quickly add expenses and timesheets to make customer billing more efficient
- depending on permissions, ability for team members to view the latest information for the entire project, not just for their assigned tasks
- ability to know what risks the user is responsible for, their progress against a project plan, and needed mitigation steps
- ability to have a consolidated view of all scheduled tasks, so as to obtain a single view of business activity

4.5.8   Ideas and scope management

The PPM tool-set needs to enable the business to manage project scope in such aspects as ideas management, creation, categorisation, planning, forecasting, strategic fit, impact of project pipeline, capability, KPIs and performance estimates for the future. Scope management capability sets up the analytics for future planning and bid adjustments, allows for long term business monitoring, and the building of a business case for each stage of the life cycle which aids in project prioritisation and portfolio management.

4.5.9   Procurement management

Procurement management supports the procuring of external resources and project related goods. Procurement management capability within a PPM solution should provide control over contract staff and agency relationships and the ability to manage individual contract details and rates, automate the collation and acceptance of agency bills, and generate invoice accruals.

Key capabilities and features should include:

- *Agency relationship management*: The system should enable you to consolidate all of your agency details in one central repository and compare and contrast agency rates in real time across your entire organisation.
- *Contract history management*: The system should enable you to track the entire history of a contract from the contractor search and evaluation stages, to managing contract details and rates, through to tracking contractor time and expenses, approving and reconciling bills and paying agencies.
- *Centralised contractor management*: The system should enable you to manage all of your contractors as part of a single organisational resource pool, and query their skills, experience and productivity.

4.5.10 Risk management

Another key aspect of a PPM solution is the ability of the business to manage and mitigate risks. Reviewing risks across projects and programmes is essential for selecting a good mix for a portfolio. The system needs to be able to produce metrics and reports in order to outline problem areas and programmes which carry high risks. It needs to be able to take a high-level, macro view of multiple projects, to identify and quantify risk and cost value, and to select the right mix of projects.

Key components need to include:

- *Centralised risk database*: The solution needs to be able to provide for a consistent centralised risk register that helps to focus the organisation on active risk management, allowing the business to take control of key business initiatives.
- *Real-time risk reporting and analysis*: The solution needs to provide real-time risk analysis and management information reports to assist in the decision making process. The solution needs to ensure that risks can be filtered based on any predefined criteria, allowing organisation-wide analysis by risk category.
- *Mitigation support*: Having assessed risk, the system needs to be flexible enough to allow the definition of activities to support mitigation. This includes the allocation of responsibility to specific individuals. With mitigation functionality, risks can be quickly re-evaluated, allowing managers to take informed decisions and redirect resources appropriately.

4.5.11 Communications management

The PPM solution should provide the individual stakeholder within the PPM process with the ability to communicate, exchange information and develop business processes. In other words, the PPM solution needs to come with features that enable project data distribution and project intelligence gathering so that participants can collaborate, and maintain, manage and share current or previous project knowledge.

These features typically include:

- workflow management
- document management
- knowledge repositories

Communicating information about the business is important to the successful delivery of projects and programmes. A central repository of project related information, documents and communications is essential for facilitating cross-departmental and multi-team collaboration. The PPM tool-set needs to be able to give each individual the same information, up-to-date ideas, proposals, processes and so on, in order to improve interaction between all stakeholders. The required features will be discussed in more detail below.

Workflow management

Workflow management is often seen as the workhorse of PPM; it is essential that the solution be able to route documents and forms through customised, user defined workflow processes. The PPM solution needs to be able to model multiple workflows to help manage the project process throughout the entire life cycle, while enforcing the portfolio framework across the business. Workflow capability needs to be either configurable 'on the fly' or to provide out-of-the-box graphical representations of a wide variety of business methodologies.

For example, typical workflows include those relating to:

- *new product management*: graphical representation of a project, programme or product life cycle
- *ideas management*: graphical representation of ideas management steps including, for example, creation, categorisation, exploration, business case preparation, commercialisation and submission
- *portfolio prioritisation*: graphical representation for managing the following steps: idea creation, idea submission, submission review,

portfolio selection, business case review, approval, project execution and monitoring
- *basic timesheet/expense collection*: for example, graphical representation of submission to approvers and acceptance/rejection by approvers

Some of the basic key capabilities of workflow management are those of:

- creating rules using simple, user defined processes
- routing documents and forms
- creating workflow activity audit trails
- assigning approval requirements for each step in a workflow
- notifying team members when a business process hits the workflow inbox

Document management

Documents are often the heart of a PPM process, so the solution needs to come with a powerful and complete document management system, including the ability to:

- handle any type of document
- build a version history for each document, with check-out and check-in tracking
- create an audit trail including both change history and view history
- display document details, such as filename, format, size, author, current version, date last modified and whether or not the file is currently 'checked out'
- link documents to other objects, discussions, deliverables, tasks, and so on
- use a workflow to route documents for review or approval
- control access using detailed, role based and user based security protocols
- associate document-specific discussion threads with each document, allowing participants with appropriate permissions to consolidate commentary around a particular document

Knowledge repositories

A relatively new addition to the PPM tool-set are knowledge repositories, or what is more commonly termed a centralised discussion thread. This allows project stakeholders to consolidate thoughts and ideas and share running commentary with other project participants. Typical knowledge repositories allow the user to see who posted a discussion comment and who has read the user's previous comments.

Key components need to include the ability to:

- attach documents and link other project objects to a discussion message
- track who has read each message
- hold discussions around specific documents

4.5.12   Governance management

The PPM solution allows for the development of governance dash-boards (see section 4.5.7 on role based dashboards), guiding users to essential, governance related activities, documents and information. The solution needs to provide for the creation of business plan models allowing for governance work and ensuring all audit milestones are met, helping to keep the business on track. Thanks to governance management, process and activity performance improvement is aided through the measurement and tracking of project or activity related data, whereby baselines can be set and analysed to track performance improvements.

4.5.13   Quality management

Quality management capability needs to provide for guided workflow using standardised templates, project knowledge, corporate or industry standards, project models and defined process efficiency measurements and metrics to ensure quality, consistency, and efficiency of executed projects and their deliverables.

4.5.14   Integration management

It is essential that the PPM tool-set come with open database technology (commonly refereed to as Open Database Connectivity, ODBC) that helps ease integration into third-party systems. These integration features should come as standard and include the following key components:

- integration with third-party applications which should be available either out-of-the-box or through customisation, with products from Microsoft, Oracle, and so on

- integration of data on project planning, execution and change with project deliverables via a project planning methodology and a change authorisation system
- ability to manage pipelines (external opportunities or internal prospects) and maintain a list of contacts and communications; for external customers, it allows for lead qualification, tracks sales opportunities and forecasts potential revenue
- support for project management methodologies such as PRINCE2 as well as business change methodologies such as Six Sigma and CMMI, aiding in data capture and monitoring within the framework

CHAPTER 5

Build a PPM framework

5.1 Key PPM infrastructure challenges

Where do we start, and what is the makeup of the PPM process? In this chapter we will take a high-level view of the PPM framework and discuss its various component areas. While discussion here is designed to introduce and build a basic familiarity with the PPM process, Part III, comprised of Chapters 7 to 11, will explore the process's mechanics in greater detail. We also examine in later chapters how the PPM process is successfully delivered into the business, how to utilise best practice methods to execute the process and how to embed it into the organisational culture to ensure sustainability and longevity.

The framework discussed below takes into account the fact that every business is different and possesses its own idiosyncrasies. We recommend that the framework be used as a baseline; the different phases and steps will need to be morphed in different ways to suit the nature of your business.

Delivering a workable PPM process is a difficult challenge. The implementation of a poorly defined method is as bad as, if not worse than, not implementing any form of process to control project delivery.

When implementing a PPM process the business is confronted with these typical challenges:

- Disparate project and resource registry and information gives management an insufficient basis for making tough decisions. Much of the information required to make project selection decisions is therefore at best uncertain and at worst very unreliable. The result is that no one wants to be the one to kill a questionable project.
- Poor portfolio definition and missing strategic criteria mean that projects are typically a poor fit with strategy and overall spending does not reflect the strategic priorities of the business.
- Many companies suffer from poor project selection and prioritisation criteria. This leads to too many mediocre projects finding their way

into the pipeline. Those few good projects that do exist are usually starved of resources, end up taking too long to market and failing to achieve their full potential. The result is too many low risk and low value projects.

- Typically many PPM processes have poor traffic-light criteria for 'go/kill/hold/fix' decisions. As a result, projects are simply added to the 'active list' with no clear directional focus and little or no understanding of their impact on the business.
- There is also a limit on the amount of resources within a business and how they are allocated across the organisation's projects. A decision to fund a project may mean that resources must be taken away from another, and resource transfers between projects are not totally seamless. Even when a large project does get started, available resources get sucked into it, often leaving other projects high and dry.
- Implementing PPM naturally results in hierarchies. Hierarchies have a tendency to breed bureaucracies, so companies naturally interested in building a PPM infrastructure must find a balance between circulating top-level strategy throughout their structure and restricting workflow with red tape. Overly rigid and complex structures that tie your projects down risk choking off innovation that comes from the bottom up.

5.2   Component areas of the PPM framework

Effective PPM analysis involves measuring and comparing portfolio business results to determine whether the portfolio is meeting its objectives, as defined by the business decision criteria and portfolio definition. The assessment process needs to incorporate both a short and a long term perspective, and should measure and examine both tactical and strategic parameters. These include:

- *tactical portfolio parameters*: condition, health and performance of the individual projects
- *strategic portfolio parameters*: overall portfolio results and impact on the business's strategic objectives

The management of an effective PPM framework is about the selection and prioritisation of projects to deliver the highest value, based on the pre-established portfolio business definition and criteria. The definition and priorities need to be based on both individual project benefits and the overall impact on the project portfolio. In addition, the resulting portfolio mix must not exceed the organisation's resource capacity or capability.

A PPM framework needs to be designed to map the health/contribution data for each project onto the business decision criteria and needs to empower managers with the ability to see whether a project is either meeting or exceeding threshold indicators, thereby identifying portions of the portfolio that are out of compliance. The portfolio dashboard as outlined in Chapter 4 (section 4.5.7) helps the PPMT to interpret portfolio information and analyse each project threshold as having a status of Red, Amber or Green (RAG) and then develop reports that enable them to understand the health of their projects at a glance.

PPM is a repeatable process for defining, planning, prioritising, approving and executing work as a business portfolio. The PPM framework needs to enable managers to:

- identify, qualify, and fund projects/programmes that address the business strategy
- manage organisational resource demand, capacity, and capability
- measure performance to ensure that projects/programmes are collectively meeting the portfolio strategy
- identify and take corrective actions on projects/programmes not in compliance with portfolio objectives and commitments
- balance the portfolio to ensure that the business has the right mix of short, medium and long term projects
- establish effective communication and reporting mechanisms that enable timely, fact based decision making regarding projects, programmes, and the overall portfolio
- implement a process to make continuous improvements to the portfolio

The PPM framework continually feeds back into itself (see Figure 18) and at a minimum should include the following processes:

- portfolio definition, strategy alignment and ideas management
- resource and business capability analysis
- portfolio selection, prioritisation and authorisation
- portfolio execution and monitoring

5.3 Portfolio definition, strategy alignment and ideas management

The portfolio definition process is where you define the terms, scope, domain and definition of your portfolio, and gain agreement on your basic portfolio model (see Chapter 8). It is essential to keep in mind that

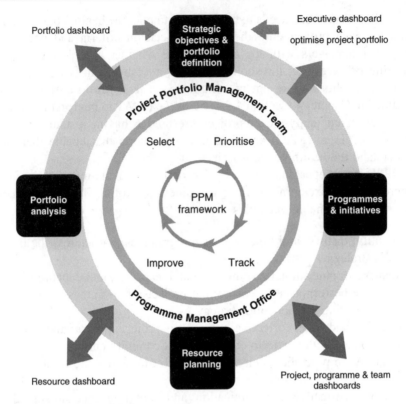

Figure 18 Sample PPM framework

the portfolio framework is a collection of projects and resources that you are managing as a group in a way that maximises the total collective business value.

5.3.1   Defining the portfolio

The types of variables that need to be considered for defining the portfolio are:

- Domain or scope of organisational coverage, that is, which business groups, units, divisions, departments and teams to include within the portfolio. Understanding the total scope will enable you to set up multiple portfolios that are more manageable; thus, you may wish to set up a portfolio definition of each major business unit or division. For example:

- o organisation-wide portfolio
- o divisional and departmental portfolios
- o multiple portfolios per organisation
- o smaller portfolios based on scope of work
- Scope of work included within the portfolio, and a definition of the categorisation scheme (see Figure 19). For example, does a project (a) support business processes and administration such as IT or finance; or does it (b) control services; or does it (c) directly grow the business through sales and marketing; and/or does it (d) drive the business through R&D or new product development?
- It is important from the outset to define the portfolio's key performance indicators (KPIs) and types of scoring models. It is impossible to compare apples with apples if the various project justifications are based on conflicting models. You need to understand the models that your organisation wants to utilise and make sure all projects are justified using those models. Most organisations are driven by financial or cost measures, such as profit, sales, net present value (NPV), internal rate of return (IRR), or earned value analysis (EVA). Although financial metrics are extremely important and directly impact the bottom line, other key criteria should be included, such as a balanced score card, and cost/benefit analysis. The choice of model is also important and will depend very much on the type of organisation, and the composition of the portfolio(s) (see section 5.5 on portfolio selection for more detail on the types of methods).

5.3.2 Defining strategy alignment

Decisions on project selection and prioritising cannot be taken without knowing what the company or organisation feels is important. The value that a project brings to your business is based on the cost/benefit implications and how well it aligns with your organisation's goals and strategies.

- Mandatory
- Strategic
- Business support
- Experimental
- Infrastructure
- Maintenance
- Cross-organisational

Figure 19 Types of portfolio categories

Therefore the definition process needs be to carefully embedded and reviewed against a series of short, medium and long term strategic objectives.

What are strategic objectives? In their simplest form, strategic objectives are high-level statements that describe what your organisation is trying to achieve and how you plan to achieve it (see Figure 20). If you do not have organisational goals and strategies, you cannot evaluate projects for alignment. Moreover, if the project does not help you accomplish your goals, you may be wasting your resources.

Defining your businesses objectives and strategic alignment criteria is typically achieved by looking at where your organisation is today – a *current state assessment* – and where you want to be in the future – a *future state vision*, then determining how best to get there – a *gap analysis*. This process results in the validation (or creation) of your mission, vision, strategy, goals and objectives. In particular, your strategy and goals will provide the high-level direction that will help align and prioritise all the work for the coming business cycle.

Defining your business goals and strategies can typically be achieved by implementing the following process:

1 *Current state assessment or 'what is'*: Without a clear understanding of your organisation today, it is very difficult to put the other pieces into place. Current state assessment tells you about your organisation today, describes your organisation's mission, vision, work processes, products, services, customers, stakeholders, values, and so on.

2 *Future state vision or 'what should be'*: This includes asking the same types of questions about where your organisation should be in five years in terms of its capabilities, culture, products, services, and so on.

3 *Gap analysis or 'how to'*: This forms the basis of the portfolio selection process and determines those projects that will be for consideration. Gap analysis highlights all the necessary steps to get from your current state to your future state. The result of the gap analysis is a short term and long term strategic plan that describes the things that need to happen to move you toward your future state. These initiatives give you the foundation that you need to make rational decisions on the things that are important and the types of work that are more valuable than others. One of the purposes of the gap analysis is to define a set of projects to close the gap and move you toward your desired state.

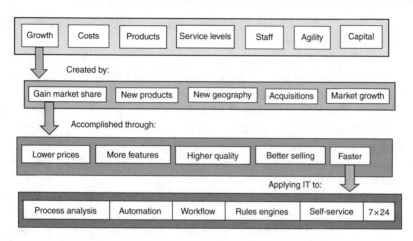

Figure 20 Strategic objectives and how to achieve them

5.3.3 Ideas management

Carving the future vision of your organisation is inexorably linked to the development of new ideas for new products and services; however, bringing them to market is extremely challenging. PPM has become the essential management discipline to enable organisations to create frameworks for idea generation – whether this is adding new or rescoping old projects. The PPM process needs to have the capabilities for systematic idea management and concept (or business case) evaluation in order to continually evolve the 'future state' vision of the business and also to ensure misaligned projects are able to be replaced by new initiatives. The PPM process enables the business to frame ideas, assess their impact on your existing pipeline, create multiple 'what if' scenarios to determine the optimal impact on the portfolio, and balance overall demand for resources across the entire portfolio.

When new ideas surface, the typical steps for managing this process include:

- *creation*: capturing suggestions and ideas for new products from all possible touch-points (sales, service, resellers, partners, customers, consumers, marketing, and so on)
- *categorisation*: ensuring idea follow-up and assessment by the appropriate business owners, such as the business developer for a specific category
- *consolidation*: developing a repository to collect documentation and information related to the product idea

- *exploration*: sharing ideas and undertaking feasibility assessments with relevant project stakeholders
- *ensuring strategic fit*: making sure a business idea fits into the overall strategy and is feasible in terms of legal considerations, standards, and time and resource restrictions
- *business case preparation*: identifying the project components, constraints and risk, outlining financial considerations, and assigning deliverables, roles and processes for delivery
- *commercialisation*: identifying the appropriate set of skills, partners, channels and teams
- *technology assessment*: identifying the technical feasibility of a proposed project
- *project registration*: ensuring ideas are included as part of the overall project portfolio inventory
- *submission*: feeding ideas into the project portfolio plan for selection and prioritisation

5.4 Resource and business capability analysis

Many portfolio management methods do a poor job of resource balancing. Projects are evaluated, 'go' decisions are made, but resource implications are often not adequately, and what is even more important, realistically addressed. Many organisations simply consider individual projects one at a time and on their own merits, with little regard for the impact that one project has on the next. Failure to manage the business's resource capability leads to pipeline gridlock in which too many projects chase too few resources. Prioritisation is one thing; the capacity to deliver on these priorities is another. Therefore before we approve and execute the portfolio it is necessary to match up the project portfolio with the corresponding resource requirements. This stage is crucial to determining the business's capability to undertake the required work in order to meet the portfolio objectives.

The PPM framework needs to provide the PPMT with a controlled and predictable method of monitoring resource and business capability against the strategic planning process, in order to improve the probability of the business being able to meet time and budget targets. Assessing resource capacity is particularly challenging simply because so many organisations lack the processes to be able to effectively track how much effort is available for project work, and how much of that effort is committed to initiatives already under way. Before we explore the steps involved, it is essential to note that the portfolio mix should not exceed

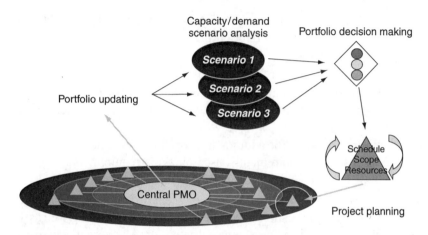

Figure 21 The PMO: driving resource supply and demand information

the organisation's resource capacity or capability. One of the central components of PPM is its ability to enable the business to implement an equitable balance between the demand and supply of resources. Figure 21 shows that, with the support of the PMO as a project knowledge centre, the PPMT is able to collect all the relevant information to update the project portfolio and build supply and demand scenarios that can then be fed back into decision making. This in turn allows the business to make the right project selections and to allocate resources to the highest priority activities across groups and organisation units.

The desired analysis can typically be achieved by implementing the following step-by-step process:

Step 1: Determine resource demand and constraints: This step looks to understand the resource spread between business-as-usual activities such as existing projects and administration, and the demands of new projects. Essential here is rooting out so-called *invisible projects* that are often buried or masked as routine work and soak up essential resources. Therefore key issues within this step include:

- identifying existing resource demands and constraints
- determining resource requirements for new projects
- analysing the ratio of resources between existing and new projects

Step 2: Create resource supply and demand scenarios: This includes analysing the impact of cancelling active projects or putting them on hold and, for example, their impact across 3, 6 and 12 month periods, as well as examining the possibility of delaying or bringing forward projects, and understanding their overall effect on the business's capacity. Key issues within this step include:

- creating portfolio variants for different allocations of resources
- developing resource redistribution scenarios and analysing their impact on the business
- determining the need for additional internal and external resources
- defining resource requirements based on skills requirements

Step 3: *Allocate resources*: As a result of scenario analysis, changes are made to the existing allocation of resources across the portfolio as well as the organisation's existing business-as-usual activities. Also essential here is to establish metrics and processes that will allow the business to determine at what point in time there will be insufficient or excess capacity for the project portfolio as a whole. Key issues within this step include:

- determining resource allocation for each project
- deciding whether to create additional internal or external capability
- ongoing capacity management in order to provide visibility of long term resource requirements

Ongoing, responsive capacity management requires constant access to up-to-the-minute data from all related systems. This allows rapid identification of changes to the project portfolio. It also enables modifications to be simulated in response to deviations and bottlenecks, ensuring that the right decisions are made. Resource and business capability analysis provides decision support for the following issues:

- Which projects can be executed with the available capacity?
- Where and how can capacity at one organisational unit be reassigned to another and how can a project portfolio be capacity-optimised?

5.5 Portfolio selection, prioritisation and authorisation

One of the most significant challenges of PPM is to understand how the portfolio of projects is selected, prioritised and approved. The primary objectives are twofold:

- to select and prioritise projects to deliver the highest value
- to ensure that there is balance in the mix of projects

It is essential that priorities be based on both individual project benefits and the overall impact of the project portfolio. Every project will be treated differently, with some flying through the selection and prioritisation process and others that simply get bogged down.

The selection, prioritisation and approval process will allow the business to address the following key issues:

- documenting a detailed inventory of projects
- developing a value ranking for each project against tactical criteria and strategic objectives
- analysing and identifying project risks vs benefits
- developing an idea of an optimum or acceptable size of the project pipeline

The project portfolio comprises projects that offer widely differing value. Projects vary by their short and long term benefit, their synergy with corporate goals and their level of investment and anticipated payback. The business needs to develop selection, prioritisation and approval processes by which it is able to evaluate projects according to their health, cost and strategic contribution to the organisation over the short, medium and long term. This part of the PPM framework process brings all the work involved together for review and scrutiny. Projects that do not surface as a part of the process will not have a chance to make it into the final list of authorised work.

The key steps involved within the selection, prioritisation and approval are highlighted in the sub-sections which follow.

5.5.1 Building a project registry

During the gap analysis phase the business builds up a list of projects. This is continued in the selection and prioritisation process in which the business builds up a project registry (see Figure 22 and Chapter 8, section 8.2) that allows it to determine the overall complexity and challenge of the portfolio. In other words, the process sets out to answer these questions:

- Is the project worth doing?
- What is achievable?
- Is there sufficient capability and capacity to do this?
- What is the impact on the business?
- What are the relative benefits of each programme/project?

- Project title
- Key personnel, for example, project manager
- Corporate objectives to which this contributes
- Priority level, for example, mission-critical, highly desirable, desirable
- Overall level of risk and impact of not delivering
- Key milestones with indicative dates
- Key partners involved in the delivery chain
- Dependencies
- Budget
- Life cycle stage
- Assessment of current status:
  - RAG status (Red, Amber, Green)
  - progress against planned milestones
  - performance against budget

Figure 22 Typical project registry information

5.5.2   Project value: scoring and prioritising

Determining a value for a given project is a crucial step. There is no single definition of the 'right' project; however, the project value must be superior to that offered by other projects. The scoring criteria used to select and prioritise projects will however be customised by the business that is implementing the PPM process. The methods that an organisation uses have a big impact not only on the projects that get chosen but also on the projects that get proposed and how they get prioritised. We now briefly explore some of the methods that are used to score and prioritise projects.

Balanced score carding methods

The balanced score card was developed in the early 1990s by Drs Robert Kaplan and David Norton of Harvard Business School. This method enables organisations to clarify their vision and strategy and translate them into action. It provides feedback around both internal business processes and external outcomes in order to continuously improve strategic performance and results. When fully deployed, the balanced score card transforms strategic planning from an academic exercise into the nerve centre of an enterprise. The majority of currently available portfolio management software tools provide the capability for defining both financial and non-financial metrics. See Figure 23.

Earned value analysis (EVA)

Earned value analysis is a measurement and management technique that integrates technical performance requirements and resource planning with schedules, while taking risk into consideration.

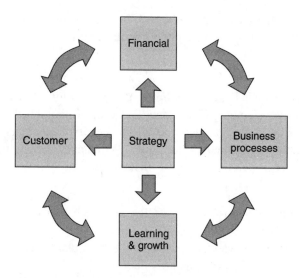

Figure 23 Kaplan and Norton's balanced score card

In other words, EVA is a management technique that relates resource planning to schedules and to technical cost and schedule requirements. All work is planned, budgeted, and scheduled in time phased 'planned value' increments, constituting a cost and schedule measurement baseline.

Earned value analysis also provides an objective measurement of how much work has been accomplished on a project. Using the EVA process, the management team can readily compare how much work has actually been completed against the amount of work it was planned to accomplish. Again, all work is planned, budgeted, and scheduled in time phased 'planned value' increments, constituting a performance measurement baseline.

Net present value (NPV)

The net present value of an investment (in this context, a project) is the difference between the sum of the discounted cash flows which are expected from the investment, and the amount which is initially invested. NPV is an effective way of expressing how much value a long term project investment will result in, and it has become an industry standard method. However, there are some limitations to NPV measurement:

- Although it is widely used for making investment decisions, it does not account for *flexibility or uncertainty* after the project decision has been made.

- NPV is unable to deal with *intangible benefits*. This inability decreases its usefulness for handling strategic issues and projects.

Cost/benefit analysis (CBA)

Cost/benefit analysis is the *weighing-scale approach to decision making*. All the positive elements (cashflows and other intangible benefits) are put on one side of the balance and all the negative elements (the costs and disadvantages) are put on the other. Whichever weighs the heavier wins. However, it can bring with it mistakes and problems:

- A frequently made mistake in the CBA method is to use *non-discounted amounts* for calculating the costs and benefits.
- Caution should be exercised with people who claim that 'if you can't measure it does not exist/has no value'.
- Especially in more strategic investments, frequently the intangible benefits clearly outweigh the financial benefits.
- Risk must often be considered as a factor in making the decision.

Other scoring and prioritisation models

Other types of models applicable to project scoring and prioritisation, as well as techniques employed to make 'go/kill/hold/fix' decisions include:

- expected commercial value (ECV)
- productivity index (PI)
- strategic buckets method
- risk-reward bubble diagram

For a full breakdown of scoring methods we recommend the excellent White Paper series written by Drs R Cooper and S Edgett of Stage Gate (see the Reference Material section at the end of this book).

5.5.3 Identifying and measuring project risks

Every project has risks, so it is essential to identify mitigation procedures and contingencies. By identifying project risks, those managing the execution process are given advance warning of problems that might arise and are able to put in place adjustment steps. For example, the risks of implementing a multi-year, multinational project, complete with major process redesign, may be quite significant. The combination of project value and risk assessment allows the portfolio to be selected in a meaningful way, and enables the PPMT to compare and prioritise competing proposals.

Key risk variables include:

- project interdependencies within the portfolio
- resource capacity/capability vis-à-vis demand
- changes in business strategy vis-à-vis operational activities
- changes in business processes that conflict with the PPM process
- governance risk in relation to board and management performance with regard to ethics, community stewardship, and company reputation
- strategic risks resulting from errors in strategy, such as choosing a technology that can't be made to work
- operational risks, including those resulting from poor implementation, or process problems such as those of production and distribution
- market risks, including in relation to competition, foreign exchange and commodity markets, interest rates, liquidity and credit
- legal risks, arising from statutory and regulatory obligations, including contract risks and litigation brought against the organisation

Identifying portfolio risks starts with an evaluation of the specific project portfolio environment. What business decision criteria have been established? What working assumptions regarding the organisation's current business processes and decision points might increase risk for the portfolio? Managers should refine this evaluation iteratively, as they plan, assess and manage their portfolio.

5.5.4 Prioritising, balancing and approving the project pipeline

By creating a 'value proposition' for each project and then evaluating projects according to their health, cost and strategic contribution to the organisation over the short and long term, the business is able to build a realistic picture of the project pipeline. Understanding project value and risk enables the business to construct a portfolio that is balanced. For example, high value projects are clearly the most sought after, but their risks, if too high, may dilute their attractiveness. Conservative projects may quell fears of losing an investment, but if the returns are too low, they may undermine the company's 'future state' vision.

It is essential to eliminate overlapping and redundant projects and select the most value-producing projects for execution, ensuring that funds are directed towards the most deserving initiatives. However, it is also important to recognise that the project portfolio will be comprised of projects that offer widely differing values but collectively strive to achieve the overall strategic objectives. Projects within the portfolio will have varying short and long term benefits, specifically as regards their synergy with corporate goals, and their level of investment and anticipated payback.

Use of scoring methods as outlined above (see also Chapter 8) will enable the PPMT to select clear criteria for how projects are to be prioritised. For example, the criteria need to include:

- support for strategic goals
- short and long term value to the business
- risk/return/future payoffs
- resource demand and impact
- financial impact
- timescale

The criteria should be defined, understood and able to be evaluated on a consistent basis from project to project. The prioritisation criteria therefore focus on both tangible and intangible benefits, allowing the PPMT to accurately measure the value of the business's projects, and determine their long term strategic orientation as well as their operational impact. Prioritisation should aggregate new project ideas and categorise existing projects as mission-critical, highly desirable or desirable in order to compare their value and level of importance to the business. There are huge differences between projects, yet too often we see a failure to recognise the differences and handle each accordingly. For example, Figure 24 shows the following types of categorisation:

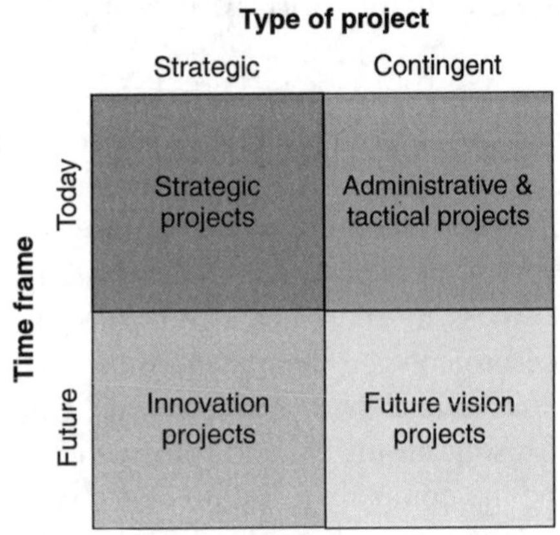

Figure 24 Categorising types of projects

- *Tactical projects* deliver competitive advantage today. They have low risk, medium-skill requirements and deliver on the existing business plan.
- *Administrative projects* deliver on currently promised service levels and support existing strategic projects. By their nature, they are low risk, low-ROI projects requiring moderate skills.
- *Strategic projects* deliver competitive advantage in the future. They have high risk, high-skill requirements and look to reduce the gap between the business's current state and its future vision.
- *Innovation projects* are smaller, experimental projects that may deliver possible competitive advantage tomorrow. They are usually high risk and often require resources that the organisation does not yet possess.
- *Future vision projects* are contingent upon strategic and innovation projects. These projects have a high risk and high-skill contingency.

Project types can also be categorised by level of importance, for example:

- *Mission-critical projects* are essential to successful delivery. If the project is not successful there are major implications for the business.
- *Highly desirable projects* are important but not essential. If the project is not successful there are serious (but not major) implications.
- *Desirable projects* are all those that do not meet the mission-critical or highly desirable criteria.

The approval step is where you determine the actual work to be funded. When this has been approved the projects concerned will then be included within the final portfolio plan. It is important to remember that the business will never have enough funding to cover all of the proposed work and that not all of the projects prioritised will be approved. After projects have been categorised, prioritised, allocated funding, and resourced, the portfolio plan is ready to be approved and should be published to the business. It is essential to publish this plan at every level within the business so that the individual stakeholders understand the importance of what they are working on and its strategic value to the business. Once the portfolio plan is in place the PPMT and the PMO manage its delivery. The PMO feeds back metrics such as costs, risk, schedules and milestones to the PPMT. The PPMT continually reassesses project performance against strategic objectives and reprioritises, adding new and terminating old projects where necessary. The PPMT also provides two-way feedback with executives, ensuring the planning cycle remains on track and aligned with the business's objectives.

5.6 Portfolio execution and monitoring

Not all projects make the grade and many need to be eliminated even after the portfolio has been approved, because:

- The projects concerned do not provide sufficient value and are no longer aligned with the business's objectives.
- Projects with a higher urgency have been proposed, resulting in a delay to or termination of current projects.
- A project has been rescoped and integrated within another.
- Technology has changed, negating the benefits of a planned project.

With only a small percentage of the proposed projects approved and executed, it is crucial that they succeed. Since the business is changing throughout the year, there will also be ongoing changes to the portfolio. This includes the addition of new projects and the elimination of old. This ongoing process of replanning and rebalancing the work, based on changing business needs, is also a part of the portfolio management execution and monitoring process. Portfolio management is therefore more than a one-time event that is performed once a year during your business planning phase. It is a continual, iterative process that needs ongoing monitoring and course correction. It is essential that the PPMT take proactive steps to resolve problems and keep projects on track by:

- correcting overlaps and redundancies
- reviewing and resolving issues and problems
- monitoring project spending and adjusting budgets
- monitoring and mitigating project risks
- managing resource conflicts such as supply and demand shortfalls
- reassessing the timing and duration of projects

The PPM selection and prioritisation process is easily emasculated if the portfolio is not actively managed. With projects straying over time, over budget and with business goals shifting and evolving, even originally well conceived projects rapidly become misaligned. However, misalignment must not be feared; it is in fact a natural and expected outcome. The real success of PPM lies in the ability of the PPMT to identify this misalignment and take corrective action. The PPMT must be able make objective 'go/kill/hold/fix' decisions and be able to recognise that a dramatic change in business priorities may eliminate the need for a project, requiring quick project termination. As stated earlier, management of the portfolio includes managing the resources, proactively communicating what is going on, reviewing and replanning the remaining work on a regular basis and measuring the results. If new projects are added to the portfolio it will mean that other, previously authorised projects will need either to be eliminated or put on hold. With the help of the PMO, the PPMT needs to document and track individual projects and implement a course correction process to ensure that the portfolio as a whole accomplishes its objective.

The typical steps involved in executing and monitoring the portfolio include:

- *Step 1*: Gathering project portfolio information
    - collecting individual project score cards
    - building a consolidated portfolio score card
    - collecting project and portfolio resource plans including shortfalls and new demands
    - building a detailed project status report
    - building a detailed portfolio status report
- *Step 2*: Measuring and analysing the project portfolio
    - measuring the performance of ongoing projects
    - measuring the success of completed projects
    - measuring interdependencies between projects
    - measuring overall business value and alignment
    - determining an inventory of projects for portfolio course correction changes
- *Step 3*: Analysing the impact of changes to the project portfolio
    - analysing the impact of projects that may be cancelled
    - analysing the impact of newly identified projects
    - analysing the impact of current projects not achieving objectives
    - analysing the impact of projects that have changed their scope
- *Step 4*: Reviewing portfolio changes and reforecasting
    - filtering new projects against the existing project portfolio
    - reviewing current and new portfolio goals and objectives
    - ensuring individual project business cases are revalidated and aligned with these objectives
    - ranking projects against revised priorities
    - updating the project inventory
    - modelling resource scenarios and analysing the overall impact on the business
    - selecting scenarios and updating the resource schedule
- *Step 5*: Communicating and implementing portfolio changes
    - revalidating business cases for existing authorised projects
    - revalidating business cases for newly authorised projects

- o issuing a new project portfolio review
- o providing guidance on changes to portfolio work
- o communicating with project stakeholders
- o agreeing a timeframe for the next portfolio review
- o making 'go/kill/hold/fix' decisions

Being able to take corrective action on projects is a key component of PPM. If a project is not meeting its objectives, it is critical to identify the root cause, develop an action plan, and then monitor and track to ensure the action is implemented and the issue is resolved. The PPMT must have the ability to intimately understand how projects in the portfolio relate to different business goals and the ramifications if either projects or business goals change. The PPMT needs to track trends and anticipate new opportunities and threats so that project stakeholders can implement measures to avoid misalignment.

CHAPTER 6

Kick-start the process

6.1 Where to deploy PPM

Having understood the relevant issues that need to be addressed in order to start organising the business for PPM, we now need to translate this into reality.

As illustrated in Figure 25, determining the location of the business's 'domain', or in other words, where to deploy the initial PPM process, is critical. Depending on your level of project management maturity, the higher up the organisation the process is to be deployed, the more challenging its implementation will be. The proof-of-benefit (PoB) process discussed later within the chapter articulates the need to prove the initial ROI at a more tactical level within the business, typically at the unit or departmental level. The rationale is to enable the business to construct, test and model the PPM process within a low risk environment as well as understand the change management issues confronting the organisation. Beyond this, the business case built around the PoB is designed to enable the business to roll out the PPM process to other parts of the business.

To de-risk the process of organising and deploying a PPM solution, it is essential to deal with 'chunks' of activity that prove the value of the solution and process from one stage to the next. Very rarely will a business have *all* the necessary internal skills to deploy a PPM process. Therefore, to deliver successful PPM and also to strengthen any existing in-house expertise, it is recommended that the organisation be in a position to recruit outside help in the form of professional consultancy services and software application vendors. We will outline the necessary steps involved in recruiting outside expertise, then we will go into how the business can kick-start the process.

The main areas for consideration include:

- readiness assessment
- requirements capture
- vendor selection process
- business case considerations

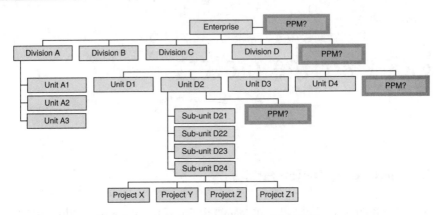

Figure 25 Determining where to deploy the initial PPM process

- the health check
- measuring the return on investment (ROI) and return on opportunity (ROO)
- establishing proof of benefit (PoB)
- building a risk management framework

Understanding the business case through to rollout within the enterprise requires that a number of stages be followed. Developing an ROI model, understanding the requirements, processes and demands involved, then putting in place a PoB all count as part of the due diligence needed for a successful implementation.

As the process progresses more detail is added to the business case, as when vendors are selected and a roadmap put in place the ROI model becomes clearer, scope changes, opportunities arise or new initiatives are derived from the initial idea.

We now provide more detail on each area for consideration in the above list.

6.2 Readiness assessment

When implementing a PPM process it is best to keep in mind the following key questions:

- *Executive sponsorship*: Are we going to get executive support to implement a Project Portfolio Management process? Will we get adequate funding, people and time to implement this?
- *Culture and organisation structure*: How flexible are the staff, can they change their existing mind-set as well as business processes?

- *Project management and business processes*: How do we tie our strategic objective to project deliverables, and what will be the impact of PPM on our existing business processes and project management infrastructure?
- *Metrics and performance criteria*: Have we established realistic, measurable performance criteria? What will be our ROI and ROO models?
- *Quick wins and credibility*: How do we ensure that we get quick wins and quick ROI? How do we ensure that PPM is taken seriously as a change management project? Are our resources going to provide us with the right inputs to go into the PPM infrastructure?
- *PPM staff and experts*: Will we have internal or external PPM experts who can manage the whole process of PPM evolution in the organisation, that is, selecting a PPM vendor, establishing success criteria, taking alternative actions if PPM implementation does not go as planned, and monitoring vendor artefacts and processes?
- *Technology*: Are our staff technically minded enough to use the software to its utmost capacity?

6.3 Requirements capture

Once an understanding of the business has been developed, the processes and demands can be mapped onto the requirements process. It is at this initial stage that high-level stakeholders should be brought into the process. The requirements capture process should itself be high-level, with a more detailed analysis done once a better understanding of what is on offer has been developed. The requirements capture process should involve the following key steps:

1 Determine requirements scope and objectives.
2 Decide on the requirements gathering model or methodology.
3 Identify the key project stakeholders.
4 Build the requirements model.
5 Gather project stakeholder needs and information.
6 Create a requirements specification, consisting of:
   o business and process requirements
   o people and resources requirements
   o capabilities and functional requirements
   o review infrastructure/IT architecture.
7 Test, review and verify the requirements specification.
8 Build the requirements into an RFI (see below).

In order to ensure best practice the following key considerations should be factored in:

- 'Translate' technical language into business language and vice versa.
- Ensure stakeholder involvement at all levels of the process.
- Draft clear and concise written documentation for all types of stakeholders.
- Ensure that the requirements are quantifiable and measurable.
- Ensure that the requirements are clearly defined in the vision and scope document.
- Prioritise requirements by their relative importance.
- Verify the completeness of the requirements by formally inspecting the documents generated.
- Identify and remove any software functionality and process steps that do not meet any of the business objectives.
- Establish and enforce a clear and realistic process for change management.
- Analyse risks to avoid unforeseen complexities and slippages.

The requirements should then be used in a preliminary request for information (RFI), typically sent to a selection of consultants and software vendors. Once the consultants and vendors have demonstrated their ability to meet a broad range of needs (any that do not meet the basics can be removed, leaving a shortlist) then the next stage is to further define the requirements in order to build a solid business case. While moving forward with the selection process there are a number of things to consider both concerning the business and while reviewing the vendors. Each vendor will take a slightly different angle on the processes and solution for implementation, which will generate value in different areas of the business. Reviewing where the biggest issues lie and who is best suited to delivering on these issues will aid in reducing the shortlist further. Without the understanding and evidence of the business case and ROI, a vendor selection may not be possible. Allowing each vendor to put forward information to gain the buy-in of the stakeholders will reduce the probability of failure later in the project.

6.4 Vendor selection process

With the initial RFI under way, a detailed list of requirements can be built up, supported by the business case and ROI model. Although meeting all the main requirements is important, it should not be the deciding factor in vendor selection. Some vendors will be able to do everything, but superiority in implementation times, costs, software functionality and process restrictions may outweigh the value of some of the other requirements. Often a detailed requirements capture is designed to understand everything available but is then mistakenly used as a bible to which all vendors should adhere. This mistake may cause software feature and process bloat, meaning that gaining actual value will be difficult and the implementation will fail. Look at the key areas of the ROI, assess which parts of the software solution and business process add most value in relation to each vendor, then a best fit across all the variables can be found. The most balanced vendor for your business needs will rarely be the one with all the bells and whistles.

Key areas to address when reviewing a vendor as part of a RFI are:

- methodology support
- process enforcement
- whether an evaluation budget is required
- whether the software is functionally supported
- integration (financials, billing, HR, and so on)
- the vendor's experience in the sector (IT, PSA, engineering, construction, and so on)
- the vendor's core values, parent company, and so on
- the business case for the solution in general and for each vendor
- ROI and ROO projections from each vendor
- feature functionality: whether the vendor promotes 'bells and whistles' or demonstrates core strengths that will add long term value to the business
- strategy: how the vendor sees the future of their technology, and business process enforcement methodologies
- where the vendor's solution comes from, how much time they have spent on it, and so on
- how the vendor's customers are supported at every stage of a partnership
- culture: whether the vendor is customer focused, part of a sales organisation, part of a PLC
- whether the vendor can provide customer references relevant to your business
- track record: where the vendor's strengths lie, their history of successful installations
- market position: whether they are market leaders, have an extensive product-set, whether PPM is a core part of their business
- partnership strategy: whether they treat the customer as a sale or more of a development partner working towards a best-of-breed solution

- focus and vision: where the vendor's focus lies in relation to their products and their future
- value added after implementation: whether they will leave, or work with you to continuously improve and develop the solution for the business

6.5 Business case considerations

Identifying the need for PPM comes from understanding how the business operates, its project management maturity level, and the processes used.

The overall objective of any PPM process is to balance project investment and expenditure across the business so that the enterprise can quickly make decisions around trusted information, aiding the change of direction within the business. In other words, the purpose of PPM is to enable the enterprise to identify projects not aligned with agreed strategy, and redirect resources to other value creation activities within the strategy. Therefore a key component of developing the initial business case is providing a breakdown of business-as-usual activities compared with project-centric activities. Doing so will allow key sponsors to understand strategic alignment issues and those projects that provide value to the corporate strategy and objectives. Management's goal should be to break up the investment into pots of tactical spend to support the strategy, making sure the spend is correctly directed into strategic value and stakeholder value coupled with shareholder value.

PPM should be delivered into the business as a change management project. The business case needs to explain how the scope of the proposed PPM project fits within the existing business strategies and develop a compelling case for change, in terms of the existing and future needs of the organisation. The business case then needs to balance the costs, benefits and risks of delivering PPM. It needs details of proposed commercial arrangements; a cost/benefit analysis ideally including analysis of 'soft' benefits, in other words those that cannot be quantified in financial terms; preferred options and any trade-offs. Also needed is an assessment of affordability and available funding linked both to proposed expenditure and to available budget and existing commitments.

The business case also needs to address 'achievability'. It needs to set out the actions which will be undertaken to support the achievement of intended outcomes, including procurement activity such as the purchase of consultancy and software. This is supported with a plan for achieving the desired outcome, identifying the key milestones, dependencies, roles, contingencies, risks, skills and experience required.

Therefore the typical business case will take the following form:

- strategic objectives and scope
- benefits realisation
- resources required:
  - technology
  - labour/skills
  - material/energy
  - infrastructure
- cultural impact
- revenue/savings
- capital and operating costs
- timescales
- appraisal:
  - investment criteria
  - funding options
  - sensitivities to uncertainty
  - risks

The development of any business case needs to address the following key issues and calculate their potential ROI and benefits:

- *People, process improvement and productivity*:
  - Improve visibility of resource allocation.
  - Improve team and individual motivation.
  - Drive more efficient business processes.
  - Free up resources to bring in other deserving projects/initiatives.
  - Bring forward revenue/cash/benefit.
  - Reduce repetition through project alignment.
- *Profitability*:
  - Embark on strategically aligned projects.
  - Drive better governance – put resource management on a professional basis.
  - Improve quality of data and decision making.
  - Reduce the risk of embarking on work that the organisation doesn't have the capacity to deliver.
- *Performance*:
  - Support priority changes quickly and effectively.
  - Manage proactively not reactively.
  - Promote good practice and consistency.
  - Extend the planning horizon to assist in strategic reviews.
  - Improve data accuracy.
  - Manage corporate planning as a business-as-usual activity.

- Enable changes to the operating model and speed up the resource allocation process.
- *Customer/partner satisfaction*:
    - Increase customer confidence and satisfaction by achieving greater accuracy in deliverables.
    - Improve collaboration by achieving predictable results, thus increasing customer trust and support.
    - Manage vendors more efficiently, enabling predictability in planning and partnering.
    - Improve communication so that third parties know where they stand.
- *Management information:*
    - Increase accuracy of management information, enabling and supporting better decision making.
    - Improve your view of organisation areas and identify people who are not busy more easily.
    - Drive accountability, improving confidence in data and decision making.
    - Encourage openness, visibility and communication of decisions.

6.6 The health check

The health check is conducted in conjunction with the selected vendor, is the first step in assessing the needs and requirements of the business, and is designed to be a low risk engagement model. The health check allows the business to analyse key processes underpinning the delivery of projects within the organisation in order to make certain that the solution and process will deliver value.

A typical health check exercise includes:

- review of a number of agreed key processes, typically including:
    - portfolio management
    - management reporting
    - project resourcing
    - milestone/delivery reporting
    - scenario modelling
    - project/programme management
    - time recording
- review of document processes, including inputs/outputs and data flows
- identification of timings for processes
- understanding and documentation of business issues and constraints

6.7 Measuring ROI and ROO

6.7.1 ROI/ROO analysis

The rationale behind any project carried out by a commercial organisation should be either to deliver cost savings, or an improvement in revenues, or both. However, it is only effectively managed projects that retain a link to strategic initiatives that can deliver on the above. Cost savings can either be delivered by a reduction in headcount, or savings gained through efficiency improvements can be used to enhance customer service, vendor management, or less tangible activities such as training, mentoring and the like.

This type of quantitative, financially based requirement for return is a very compelling driver for change, yet is only part of the overall picture when looking at both potential tangible and intangible benefits. Therefore return on opportunity (ROO) analysis helps organisations define and quantify potential top-line benefits from deploying new business processes, including in respect of revenue, market capitalisation, an increased customer base and decreased attrition. ROO analysis is most effective when it crosses departmental boundaries, integrates disparate capabilities and provides capabilities that an organisation did not have or had not addressed before.

Using an ROI/ROO calculator model is an effective way of measuring the organisation's key project and programme cost and time data to identify potential cost savings over five years.

6.7.2 Building an ROI/ROO model

Once the stakeholders have identified the common activity conducted within their control and understood the percentage split and breakdown of activity, time efficiency calculations can be made to identify the potential ROI and subsequently the ROO that are achievable. This is simply based on time savings against the 'now status' way of working and processes. These can be compared with representative savings once PPM has been implemented and adopted through an effective change programme.

Research has demonstrated that work practices without a PPM solution in place can incur a workplace productivity wastage of as much as £650 per person per month, which in turn could represent an annual wastage, within a department of 100 staff, of approximately £780,000. It is important to note that enterprises rarely cull people, but rather move savings into value creation activities such as a new or different corporate initiative.

These are the steps that need to be followed:

Step 1: Work days and staff costs

A typical ROI/ROO model will start by determining:

1 the number of working days in the year against weekends, bank holidays, annual leave, sickness
2 the cost per working day of each resource type, to include salary, benefits, employer cost, and so on, for:
   - PPMT staff (analysts, management reporting)
   - PMO staff (analysts, management reporting)
   - project/programme managers
   - project/programme delivery staff

Step 2: Project/programme related activity costs

The second element of the ROI model is largely concerned with the number of project managers and project delivery staff that will benefit from the use of a PPM solution. Therefore the next step looks to illustrate the everyday activities that both project and programme staff are normally involved with during an average week. A key issue here is to calculate the projected difference under PPM, and hence the cost savings attached to the activities performed by the different staff, and identify a potential return on investment.

For example, the model will need to determine:

1 amount of resources and their cost:
   (a) How many PMO staff do you have?
   (b) How many project/programme managers do you have?
   (c) What amount of resources do they manage?
2 resources time/effort spent on key activities:
   (a) PMO staff time/effort spent on activities such as:
       (i) project status reporting
       (ii) milestone reporting
       (iii) resourcing
       (iv) 'what if' scenario modelling
       (v) management information reporting
   (b) project/programme management time/effort spent on activities such as:
       (i) project status reporting

      (ii) task based project management
     (iii) milestone reporting
     (iv) resourcing
      (v) 'what if' scenario modelling
     (vi) project/programme management

(c) project/programme delivery time/effort spent on activities such as:

       (i) time recording
      (ii) expense management
     (iii) reduction in margin of error
     (iv) milestone achievement reporting
      (v) work scheduling, prioritisation/reprioritisation
     (vi) weekly progress and assignment meetings
    (vii) change management
   (viii) use, modification or analysis of MS Project
     (ix) cross-training required when not allocated to correct tasks
      (x) general project delivery work
     (xi) project status reporting
    (xii) task based project management
   (xiii) milestone reporting
   (xiv) resourcing
    (xv) 'what if' scenario modelling

3 overall cost savings:

(a) potential annual cost savings for PMO staff
(b) potential annual cost savings for project management staff
(c) potential annual cost savings for managed staff

Step 3: Calculating potential ROI

The next step is to determine the potential cost savings when they are netted off against the costs of software purchase and PPM implementation services. The calculation of return within the first year offsets the time taken for implementation and realisation of benefits (six months is the time estimated to begin realisation of cost/benefit). The calculation in years 2–5 includes ongoing system support costs (both annual support and internal administration costs) and any possible external consulting requirements. These time savings are then calculated as monetary values and expressed through a five-year ROI scenario, expressed as a net present value over five years (the discounted cash flow value is estimated at 15 per cent). Thus the overall costs savings can be determined by:

- potential annual cost savings for PMO staff
- potential annual cost savings for project management staff

- potential annual cost savings for all managed staff
- proposed cost of software purchase for PMO, project managers and resources
- proposed professional services to implement PPM
- internal costs to assist implementation of PPM

Step 4: Calculating potential ROO

The final step is to calculate a return on opportunity, where the time saved by the implementation of the solution is directed to more value added activities such as:

- people – improve team performance, more training, more mentoring
- process – consistent approach with more attention to detail
- productivity – more delivery of projects on time and within budget
- profitability – no budget overruns, increased customer facing resource
- performance – more streamlined processes, less hours on time and expense capture and reporting, more hours on project tasks
- partners – more customer satisfaction
- management reporting – real-time visibility, accountability and dashboard reporting

6.8　Establishing proof of benefit (PoB)

6.8.1　What is proof of benefit?

A proof of benefit (PoB) is in effect a configurable test environment that enables the business to understand from a real-world perspective how PPM will be delivered into the business. The PoB brings together the software application and processes into one single environment. As discussed in Chapter 4, the software side of the PoB can be hosted as part of an SaaS offering. This will obviate the need for an internal server installation, thus reducing costs and timescales.

The PoB exercise will involve:

- developing and agreeing PoB objectives and scope, that is, roles and responsibilities, critical success factors, timeframes and the place (or domain) in which the PoB will be conducted, in other words, the area of the business under assessment
- agreeing the issues concerning the existing status of the current processes, such as:

- o time recording
- o milestone management
- o project management
- o resource management
- o management information production
- o scenario and project modelling
- agreeing the framework for the delivery of the PoB around areas where the business can develop a PPM model and deliver it into the business
- assessing and testing the PPM model within and delivering the results back into the business

6.8.2 A PoB step process

A PoB will typically involve the following key steps.

Step 1: Objectives and goals

This step involves:

- developing and agreeing the purpose of the PoB
- agreeing and developing a timeframe for PoB delivery
- identifying and engaging key stakeholders responsible for the PoB
- targeting and defining the business domain in which the PoB will take place, that is, which departments, business units, and so on
- identifying high-level analysis of current workstreams and processes within the business domain ready for 'current state' assessment
- developing and agreeing a project structure and a governance structure appropriate to the successful delivery of PoB, wherever possible utilising existing structures, for example: roles, responsibilities, resources, project frameworks, and so on

Step 2: Principles and scope

This step involves agreeing:

- roles and responsibilities within the PoB
- key issues and risks including the management principles relating to risk and issues resolution, and development of a risk log and an issues log
- financial control and reporting mechanisms
- the prioritisation process
- quality assurance

- provision of management information, executive reporting and programme reporting
- standards
- escalation routes and procedures

The modus operandi should utilise existing processes where appropriate.

Step 3: 'Current state' assessment

This step commences the actual PoB work and looks to map out a 'current state' assessment by coming to understand the current processes within the targeted domain or areas within the business. This assessment forms the baseline from which a PPM model is built.

This step involves:

- establishing and agreeing the facts concerning the existing status of the current processes within the business, typically including attention to:
  - time recording processes
  - resource management processes
  - project management
  - programme management
  - milestone management
  - management information production
  - scenario and project modelling
  - processes and measurement criteria
  - roles and responsibilities
  - workstreams and supporting plans
  - technical architecture
  - critical project dependencies
  - resourcing requirements and constraints
  - ongoing issues and risks
- populating the ROI/ROO tool with accurate/up-to-date data ready to assess the benefits of PPM

Step 4: 'Future state' assessment

This step defines and builds a picture of the targeted PPM model, in other words, a model of what the business should be doing to benefit from PPM and how to deliver it into the business.

This step involves:

- agreeing critical success factors for the PoB and feeding PPM benefits into the ROI/ROO calculator

- defining the target PPM model, by reference to:
  - strategy and accountability processes
  - project life cycle processes
  - portfolio management processes
  - milestone management processes
  - budgets and costing processes
  - programme management processes
  - resource management processes
  - management information processes
  - scenario modelling processes
  - time recording processes
  - roles and responsibilities
- establishing and agreeing a practical and achievable PPM delivery model by mapping out process implementation and installation of the software procedures
- identifying and creating a configuration document that supports the agreed processes and maps out the overall future state assessment

Step 5: 'Gap analysis' assessment

This step looks at what the target domain needs to do to achieve a successful implementation of PPM. It involves implementing the model developed at step 4, and starts to model the PPM environment. The results of the modelling are rolled up to the executive level so as to understand the implications of a larger-scale rollout. Wherever possible, 'quick wins' should be identified, and progress made in accordance with appropriate project control and development standards and resource and budget constraints.

This step involves:

- undertaking and documenting a 'gap analysis' between the 'current state' assessment and the 'future state' assessment
- identifying and defining workstreams from the gap analysis
- developing a model and prototype processes and solutions to identify areas of improvement, and then implementing these processes and solutions
- documenting change management issues
- calculating the actual ROI/ROO of PPM implementation

Step 6: Presenting the results to the business

It is recommended that the executive sponsor be asked to deliver the PoB to the business. The findings of the PoB need to be well documented, and all key stakeholders need to be educated on all aspects of the PoB. The findings of the PoB should also be used as the basis for rollout to other parts of the business.

This step involves presenting:

- the PoB objectives
- the identified PoB target domain
- the 'current state' assessment findings
- the 'future state' assessment findings
- the 'gap analysis' assessment findings, including:
  - the defined PPM model
  - the ROI and ROO for the business
  - the change management issues
  - the process changes to be involved in rollout within the business
  - the software products needed to support rollout within the business

6.9 Building a risk management framework

Quantifying the benefits and savings at the start of the process, at the same time identifying and resolving the issues and risks associated with implementing a PPM process and solution in your organisation, will contribute to the ultimate success of the project. You need to know that the solution is 'fit for purpose' and will actually solve your business problems – not add to them! You want to prove that the benefits and savings will work for your business, technologically, economically and culturally, prior to possible procurement and deployment.

Technological questions may include:

- Does the proposed system work fast enough?
- Does it run effectively using your infrastructure?
- How easy will it be to transfer data?
- Does the software tool interface with your existing systems?

From the cultural viewpoint, you will need to answer questions like these:

- Will people find the software tool easy to work with?
- Does it mirror your established or proposed new procedures?
- Does it use familiar terminology?
- Does it fit within your project management maturity environment?

Answering these questions using traditional evaluation techniques is extremely difficult. Therefore, proactive management of risk is critical, and it is important that the PPM process develops a framework for this. Since the PPM deployment is a change management project in itself, we recommend implementing a project based risk management framework.

We define within the framework the possible events or circumstances that can have negative influences on the project. Its influence can be on the schedule, the resources, the budget, the scope and/or the quality. An essential element of this is putting in place a contingency plan that can reduce or eliminate the risks.

The factors that need to be considered when assessing project based risk include the following:

- identification – choosing unique identifiers for referring to the same risk in company or project documents
- description – the nature of the risk and how it could become a liability
- risk status – categorising the risk as new, ongoing or closed
- effect – assessing the possible consequences if the risk were to become a liability
- precautions – considering what can be done to prevent the risk becoming a liability
- contingency – drawing up plans or procedures for handling a liability if it materialises
- risk escalation – estimating the probability of the risk becoming a liability
- schedule impact – estimating the consequences of a liability in terms of time for the project

Here are the typical steps to help manage project based risk:

- planning how risk management will be carried out for the particular project – to include risk management responsibilities, activities, tasks, and budget
- assigning a risk officer – a team member, other than the project manager, responsible for foreseeing potential project problems
- maintaining a live project risk database – each risk entry should have the following attributes: opening date, title, short description, probability and importance; optionally, each risk can have an assigned person responsible for its resolution and a mitigation timeframe

- creating an anonymous risk reporting channel – each team member should have the possibility of reporting a risk that they foresee in the project
- preparing mitigation plans for those risks for which the decision to mitigate has been made – to cover what, when, how and by whom action will be taken to avoid or minimise the consequences if the risk becomes a liability
- summarising planned and faced risks, effectiveness of mitigation activities and resources expended on risk management

PART III

Execute and control Project Portfolio Management

Part I explored the definition of PPM and identified the pains in PPM. Part II discussed in detail the preparation and organisation required for the deployment of a PPM process, and the technology required in supporting the implementation.

In Part III we review in detail a step-by-step guide to the execution of the PPM process. We strongly advocate that the execution of the PPM process needs to be managed as a change project. We reiterate that strong leadership is needed to champion this change project, and that communication plans need to be in place to influence stakeholders throughout the implementation stage.

CHAPTER 7

Establish corporate visibility and environment

7.1 Managing PPM as a change project

Continuous change is the only constant that will ring a bell with those who are in business today. The META Group study showed that 50 per cent of Global 2000 companies adopted some form of project portfolio management. Yet less than 10 per cent of the companies' execution drove the portfolio value up by as much as 30 per cent, while each of the other attempts became just another failed project!

The execution of PPM has to be managed not only as a project, but as a *change management* project. Our own experience has shown that introducing the PPM process is a business process change initiative; as a result, the leadership involvement and cultural change expected from the stakeholders are fundamental to the successful implementation of the portfolio process.

There are many good texts available on managing change in organisations, so we will not attempt to rehearse them here. We will confine ourselves to two considerations. First, to highlighting Egan's model of change scenarios, shown in Figure 26, which involves generating action that produces valued outcomes or results for the organisation. Planning for change is important, but only if it leads to valued, organisation-enhancing outcomes. The valued outcome of introducing a PPM process must be well rehearsed by the project portfolio management team (PPMT), and a detailed communication plan to obtain buy-in from stakeholders must be prepared before the execution stage. In the execution of the PPM process we need to ensure that managing change among our users and stakeholders is uppermost in our implementation strategy.

Second, there are many different models and ways of looking at organisational change and the role of a change leader. The role of a portfolio sponsor is to be a change leader. To support our approach to implementing the project portfolio process as a change project, we encourage

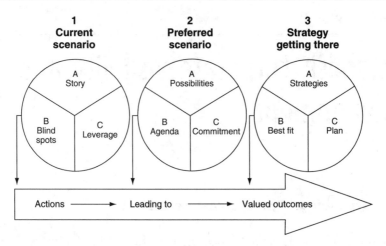

Figure 26 Change management scenarios

organisations to look at a model drawn from the work of management writer Ralph Stacey (1997). See Figure 27.

The value of this model is to help you identify where your change project lies in relation to the two dimensions of 'agreement' and 'certainty'. This in turn will help you to define the most appropriate leadership and management skills to use.

Our experience has shown that when you prepare and organise the PPM solution as discussed in Part II of this book, the project will tend to be in quadrant 1 of Figure 27, and at worst in quadrant 2. If there are no

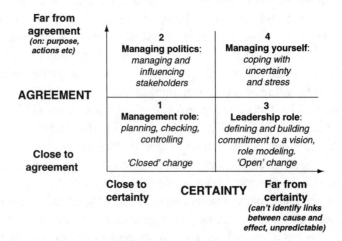

Figure 27 Understanding change

proper preparation and organisation, then you can rest assured that the implementation will be another failed project due to lack of understanding on leading change.

As a result, change leaders need to grasp what type of change they are dealing with in order to understand how best to lead it. The use of this model may also help you to decide how much emphasis you wish to give to building a shared vision and how much time to the deliverables and objectives of the portfolio change project.

7.2 Managing the project portfolio environment

The project portfolio environment suggests the application of a well defined process that allows for both flexibility and discipline. An organisation's environment is characterised by:

- uncertain and changing business information
- fluid opportunities, requiring a quick response
- multiple organisational goals and key strategic issues
- interdependencies within and between projects and programmes
- multiple decision makers across different locations

PPM needs to operate within a very challenging business environment. Severe business environmental issues include:

- intense competition
- scarce/constrained resources
- demanding customers
- time-to-market concerns
- shareholder quest for immediate returns
- long term actions are required, but short term results are the benchmark
- disconnects between strategies and operational results

When we look at the environment up close we need to consider a framework to assess the factors which may affect the management of the portfolio. Traditionally, organisations have tended to assess technical, financial, legal, economic and political factors. However, a key environment concern is integrating executive decision making with the balancing of key project dimensions. Portfolio management can benefit the organisation as a whole, but there are times when the specific environmental conditions of one business unit warrant special treatment.

The project portfolio process is the key to addressing the challenging characteristics of the business environment which create both the need for a portfolio process and the organisational inertia to resist the process. The management of the portfolio is a fundamental role of leadership and it cannot be delegated. In addition, the portfolio process links the organisation's strategy to its operational performance. As a result the process clearly identifies the strategic priorities of the organisation through critical decisions of resource utilisation.

In addition, the portfolio management environment consists of perspectives, process relationships, organisational relationships and project demand. Although the portfolio management process can be set out in a stand-alone document, it must consider and pull pieces from each of these other aspects of the environment.

Providing the programme and resource information required to support programme management, project management, functional management and portfolio management can be challenging and confusing since the same basic information is viewed and used in different ways by the various groups and levels within an organisation. Although it may appear to be a considerable duplication of effort, none of the groups involved can function properly without receiving data in the appropriate format. It is important to keep in mind and to support the information requirements of each of these groups.

Figure 28 illustrates the relationship between the three process areas that drive and sustain the portfolio management process: business strategy/marketing, the system development process and the project

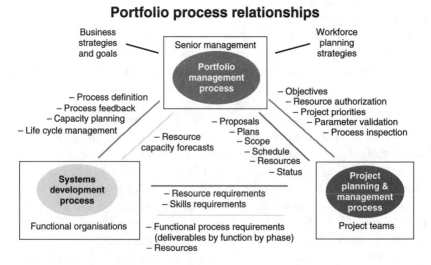

Figure 28 Portfolio process relationships

management process. These three elements comprise a dynamic environment, which requires the cross-process sharing of data. Each process makes its contribution by creating and/or updating vital strategic, product, and project (schedule, scope, and resource) information throughout the life of a project.

Project identification and initiation are typically the result of the business strategy process. The portfolio management process is intended to drive project specification and prioritisation via business goals, objectives, opportunities and strategies. Projects with the highest value to the organisation must be identified, initiated, and brought to a successful conclusion. Throughout the life of a project the business case (cost/benefit, feasibility, market attractiveness, strategic value) must be re-evaluated (or reconfirmed) as additional funding is allocated for each successive stage of the project.

Senior managers serve as 'process architects' by determining, pushing out to the organisation and enforcing the appropriate processes (and process improvements) to successfully manage the strategic interests of the organisation.

Credible project planning and definition are essential to the portfolio management process. The minimum elements necessary in order to provide the information required for effective portfolio management are:

- project schedules (work breakdown structure, with duration estimates and dependencies)
- the resource requirements to complete individual project tasks
- phase start and end dates
- dates for deliverables
- reliable communication of project information among stakeholders
- periodic project status and resource forecast updates
- a document repository containing project documents, templates, and artifacts

The system development process (SDP) typically fits within the larger context of a phase-gate process (discussed in the next section). It defines the deliverables and processes for system development projects. It identifies critical development phases and deliverables, dependencies between deliverables and/or departments, individual and/or departmental roles and responsibilities, gates, and requirements to pass through phase-gates.

The SDP provides a clear and logical sequence for producing project deliverables and for passing from one phase or stage to the next.

The phases reflect a natural progression of work across all functions involved. The SDP provides functional managers with clearly defined targets against which to allocate resources. Successful completion of SDP milestones provides the management team with the data to make fact based decisions.

In summary, the PPMT's process activities must be integrated with other, existing processes, with its interdependent relationships existing within and between product/service development processes and project management processes.

In establishing corporate visibility, our approach needs to consider four main tasks:

- *Determining the levels of project organisation*: The first step in establishing an environment that supports effective portfolio management is the explicit determination of the hierarchy of project-centric decision making.
- *Creating the PPMT*: A team is developed to assure that project work at each level of project organisation is closely aligned with the strategies of the business.
- *Defining roles and responsibilities*: The parameters of authority of the PPMT are formally defined, documented and validated to ensure that the overall project organisation understands the role of the PPMT. This facilitates the effective implementation and ongoing exercise of the PPMT's project leadership role.
- *Establishing the PPM framework*: The general process for managing the project portfolio should be made more operational by multiple supporting or framework processes that will be performed numerous times throughout the overall Project Portfolio Management process. These framework processes facilitate the efficient administration of the individual practices that ensure understanding and compliance with the overall PPM process.

7.3 Determining the levels of project organisation

As a first step we need to determine the project organisation levels. Here we need to identify the organisational infrastructure for managing project activities, determine the targeted level of project portfolio focus and gain leadership commitment to managing work through a project portfolio process.

7.3.1   Analysing the organisation's funding hierarchy

Within the organisational infrastructure, analyse how projects are funded in the organisation. Investigate the budgeting and funding hierarchies, as they may serve as good indicators of the organisation's project infrastructure, and identify the different types of approaches the company uses in funding. These may include the following:

- product/service line
- geographical responsibilities
- customer/industry type
- project/programme basis
- traditional business unit legacy

Quite often, when organisations document their structure it tends to be from a reporting authority viewpoint; however, in many circumstances this is not the same as recording from the funding/resourcing perspective. In determining project funding practices, ask the following questions and document the funding hierarchy (see Figure 29 for an example):

- What funds are included (project versus non-project)?
- Who makes funding/resourcing decisions?
- How are these decisions made?
- How do projects request funding/resources?
- When are projects funded/resourced?
- Who actually owns the funds/resources?
- How does project funding align with the budgeting process?

Another way of looking at the portfolio hierarchy is by evaluating the framework around which the processes and relationships described above support PPM. The portfolio sub-structure can be comprised of domains, programmes and projects as shown in Figure 30.

Domains are spawned by business strategy. They enable projects to be grouped or partitioned based on strategic significance to the organisation, for example, 'strategic/enterprise' (IT portfolio), 'new products', 'infrastructure', 'maintenance', 'cost reduction' and so on. Programmes are allocated to domains based on how well they meet domain criteria. It is possible for a programme to qualify for more than one domain, for example, it could be a 'strategic/enterprise' programme or a 'new product' programme. Once programmes are allocated to the appropriate domains, they are prioritised and broken down into projects.

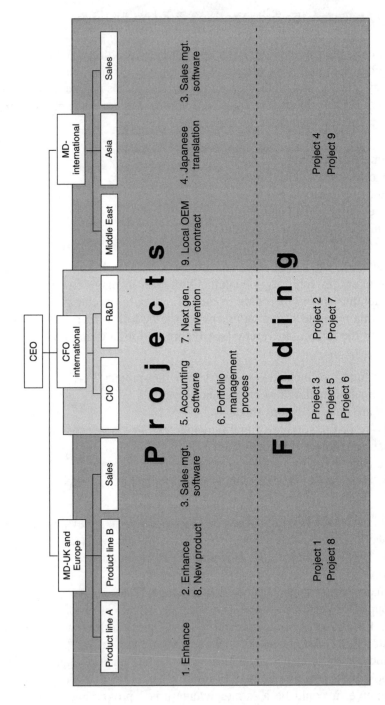

Figure 29 Project funding hierarchy (example)

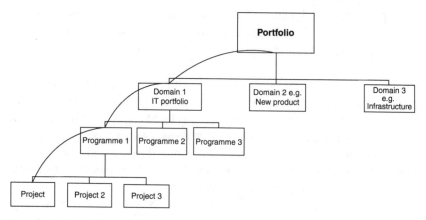

Figure 30 Portfolio sub-structure

7.3.2 Determining the appropriate PPM structure

Another key to determining the correct application of PPM is a clear and commonly held understanding of how the organisational structure itself supports the management of project activities. For instance, the company can be a market driven organisation, with each business unit supporting a product or service line or the infrastructure, as shown in Figure 31.

The portfolio management structure should reflect the strategic emphasis of the organisation. In order for the project portfolio to be effective, PPM should occur at many different levels within the organisation. With the different levels, care must be taken to ensure that strong leadership commitment exists at the targeted level. For the portfolio process to be meaningful it needs to be translated into specific resource

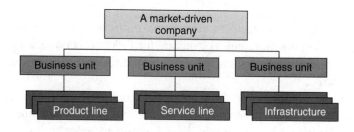

A project portfolio can be managed at each level

Figure 31 Portfolio management structure

utilisation at the project level. The strategic impacts of portfolio decisions are more readily visible at higher levels within the organisation; balance is the key. You need to decide at which levels PPM will operate in the organisation.

In the multiple tiers of PPM application, the uppermost tier must carry the strongest priority – its resource commitments are honoured first. After fulfilling the resource requirements of the top level, the remaining available resources can be managed through a portfolio process at the supporting levels. In order to ensure buy-in and commitment throughout all tiers of application, membership of the PPMT should include representation from subordinate tiers.

7.3.3 Validating with the executive management team

To ensure continued involvement of the executive management team, validation of the process must be conducted. This will also measure the level of commitment of that team. We have seen validation occurring at each targeted level of the project portfolio with the appropriate management team. As the full executive team is unlikely to serve as the PPMT, validation helps promote common understanding.

At this point, validation is focused on the organisational levels targeted for the project portfolio process. This initial validation should also address the willingness of the executive team to manage resources and project priorities through the application of a project portfolio process.

In summary, we can identify three key tasks in determining the levels of project organisation:

- *analysing the organisation's funding hierarchy*: identifying the organisational infrastructure for providing funding of project work, and guidance in determining the appropriate project portfolio leadership structure
- *determining the appropriate project portfolio management structure*: documenting the hierarchical structure for PPM decision making based on the funding infrastructure, to ensure common understanding and consensus
- *validating the portfolio management structure with the executive management team*: reviewing the project organisation document with the executives who approve project funding in order to gain leadership commitment to managing project work through a project portfolio process

7.4 Creating the PPMT

The setting-up of the PPMT clarifies the roles and responsibilities of the members and ensures the involvement of all the team members necessary for project portfolio success. It also gains organisational commitment.

7.4.1 Determining and assigning project portfolio sponsors

The PPMT needs to know who its sponsor is. We have seen PPMT members who did not know. If you as a PPMT member do not know who your sponsor is, you need to determine this. The sponsor should ideally be one person; in any event, select or create an executive sponsor with final decision making authority. For example, in our dealings with an aerospace company, we found that although they had a sponsorship team, the fact that there was no single line of authority to make decisions gave rise to conflicting messages and hidden agendas, leaving the PPMT at a loss to get the work done.

A sponsor typically sets the direction, obtains resources and approves the project plan. The appointment of a portfolio sponsor sends a powerful message to the organisation about the importance of the project portfolio process. Finally, the sponsor must be a strong advocate for the benefits of the project portfolio, a true believer.

Some of the successful traits of a sponsor can include the following:

- is influential
- is at senior level
- is process oriented, or a gatekeeper
- endorses project management
- is a coach
- is persistent
- is an evangelist for the PPM approach

We can summarise the portfolio sponsor's role as follows:

- providing official backing, resources, and strategic direction for the PPMT
- providing a focal point for decisions beyond the PPMT's scope of authority
- appointing the portfolio manager
- approving all portfolio decisions, validating where appropriate and recommending changes where needed

- ensuring organisational buy-in
- resolving escalated conflicts
- communicating strategic business decisions/issues to enable the PPMT to maintain an appropriate portfolio

7.4.2 Determining and assigning the PPMT

The PPMT leader heads the portfolio team, and is also sometimes called the portfolio manager. The portfolio manager holds an authoritative position relative to other PPMT members, having clear empowerment from the portfolio sponsor. The appointment of the portfolio manager is made by the sponsor. This appointment needs to be formalised in writing and widely communicated. This is a full-time position. The following characteristics of a successful portfolio manager tend to be the same as those of a project manager:

- is a good motivator and team leader
- is an effective communicator
- is a good organiser
- is familiar with the business units within the target domain
- understands the project portfolio process
- is an experienced project manager
- maintains a team player attitude
- is cognisant of group processes
- is willing to face up to internal/external obstacles
- is committed to portfolio success
- is well respected by peers

The role of the selected portfolio manager includes liaison with the executive management team on project issues; responsibility for the activities of the PPMT; responsibility for developing and managing framework processes, and appointment of PPMT members. Other roles and responsibilities can include:

- coordinating the activities of the PPMT to meet the goals of the portfolio process
- ensuring complete and accurate information is collected from the projects and programmes within the domain
- defining and establishing the framework of PPMT practices
- creating and implementing periodic review processes for the project portfolio

- arbitrating and resolving conflict within the PPMT
- escalating issues to the portfolio sponsor when timely resolution has not been attained within the PPMT
- ensuring PPMT members stay committed to the process
- serving as a point of liaison between the portfolio sponsor and the PPMT

The membership of the PPMT is highly dependent on the domain and business concerns. It is best to first examine the business strategies within the domain and identify the key functional organisations and projects for representation. We normally recommend key executives within the domain of interest who exhibit leadership qualities and are strong advocates for the portfolio process. The members must be committed to the PPM process and understand the balance required between functional objectives and wider business strategies. This may sound rather trite, but in our experience we know that members who faithfully attend all PPMT meetings, who personally participate in PPMT activities, and who have not delegated their responsibilities nor allowed any stand-ins, have made PPM implementation a success.

It is important to ensure that the PPMT has adequate and appropriate representation and that its members are validated by the executive management team. This validation can provide confirmation that the PPMT membership is consistent with the business strategies of the domain.

In summary, we can identify four sub-tasks when establishing the PPMT:

- *Identifying your portfolio sponsor*: A 'champion' of the project portfolio and the resources assigned to the project portfolio is identified for each portfolio and formally appointed as the sponsor of the PPMT. This ensures that the PPM process becomes a part of doing business and provides executive-level support for the PPMT.
- *Determining and assigning the PPMT*: PPMT roles need to be determined, and members assigned to it who can represent the diverse interests of the organisation. This team manages the PPM process and authorises the deployment of resources for project work.
- *Determining the responsibilities of each PPMT member*: PPMT members collectively determine the specific responsibilities of each member, to ensure that all aspects of managing the portfolio are assigned to particular people. The PPMT roles and responsibilities are documented in its roster.
- *Validate the team roster with the portfolio sponsor* – ensure management agreement and commitment to the roles of all PPM members.

This facilitates the assumption of responsibilities by the various team members and provides for clarity and ownership of the overall responsibilities of the PMT.

7.5 Defining roles and responsibilities

7.5.1 Creating the PPMT charter

The PPMT charter is a very significant document, used to define and communicate the roles, responsibilities, and relationship to other organisational processes, of the PPMT. It is particularly useful in organisations where the portfolio process is new or unfamiliar. Thus, the charter ensures the PPMT's accountability and establishes it in its role in relation to project managers and project sponsors within each domain, formally putting the portfolio process into place.

A typical PPMT charter may be comprised of the following components:

- the PPMT mission
- the PPMT vision
- the scope of authority, with an 'is/is not' list
- the business strategy
- the critical success factors
- the measures of success
- PPMT roles and responsibilities
- PPMT activities and deliverables
- business process relationships
- standing arrangements for PPMT meetings
- the communication flow
- the change management process
- process and tools development activities
- record of the historical background

7.5.2 Defining the project portfolio role of each PPMT member

The charter will define the roles and responsibilities of each PPMT member, typically covering:

- setting criteria in accordance with business strategy
- scoring projects based on updated information
- assigning resources based on project priorities
- optimising the portfolio for greatest business impact
- continually monitoring and updating portfolio and project information
- reporting portfolio status to all concerned parties

7.5.3   Validating with the portfolio sponsor

The PPMT's charter, together with the roles and responsibilities of its members, need to be validated before establishing the framework.

7.5.4   Training the PPMT members

PPMT members and other project personnel who contribute to or are recipients of the work of the PPMT must be trained in their responsibilities as a team and individually – and as part of the PPM process. This allows the team to work together quickly and efficiently, and also ensures understanding and buy-in of the PPMT's role in the leadership of the project-centric organisation.

A training strategy should be developed based on the overriding intents and purposes of portfolio management within the organisation. At a minimum all staff should be provided with an overview of the current portfolio management goals and objectives. They should have understanding of how they fit into the grand scheme.

Staff who require training can include the project sponsors; those in functional, or product/service line areas; business unit advocates; the project portfolio sponsor; the PPMT leader, and the PMO manager. In addition, there are other portfolio participants or supporting personnel who may require training, including:

- project and programme managers
- project coordinators
- project support office members
- executive team members
- key organisational leadership
- personnel with project related responsibilities (proposal preparation, technical review, cost estimating, and so on)

It is always important to select skill based training, carried out with intact teams whenever possible; and to provide training for those directly responsible for the work and for personnel who are either contributing to or supporting the portfolio process.

Training needs have to be assessed carefully, and a training plan developed for the PPMT and supporting personnel. There is a requirement to distinguish immediate training needs (required for portfolio process implementation) from longer term training requirements that support effective management of the portfolio.

Normally, the training needs assessment is coordinated through the Human Resources function of the organisation. The PPMT and the PMO determine their own training needs with the support and guidance of the portfolio process implementation team.

The training itself can be provided from a number of internal and external sources. The PPMT should determine the preferred source(s) of the training. As a process consideration, training must occur throughout the implementation phase of the portfolio process; both formally and informally, at the start of implementation. As an ongoing consideration, training must be viewed as a continuous improvement opportunity. This must be supported by periodic assessment of the training needs of the portfolio participants and supporting personnel.

7.6   Establishing the PPM framework

The project portfolio framework is the set of procedural practices that the PPMT puts in place for the implementation and management of project portfolio process activities. The framework typically defines how the team will operate; clarifies expectations of PPMT members; and documents PPMT internal process decisions early to prevent second-guessing of team decision making processes.

Some of the benefits of the project portfolio framework can include:

- up-front determination of team practices, thereby reducing confrontation and team conflict
- well defined and widely communicated process practices, thereby lessening questions and second-guessing
- clearly articulated portfolio requirements, thereby setting expectations for all process participants
- validation of team and process boundaries, thereby promoting early discussion of PPMT roles and responsibilities

7.6.1   Determining the framework processes to be implemented

The recommended framework process can be comprised of the following categories:

- PPM implementation plan
- PPM implementation planning deliverables
- PPM implementation tracking
- alignment and coordination with organisational strategies
- alignment with other business processes and projects under way
- relationship decisions covering stakeholders, communication plan, training and escalation procedures
- decisions covering project reviews and prioritisation meetings, communication of decisions, resource estimation and turnover
- continuous process improvement

A framework checklist is given at the end of the book (Chapter 13), but is only a guide; the PPMT can of course develop its own list. It is advisable that all categories be reviewed and questions answered, normally by the portfolio manager. However, the checklist should be distributed to PPMT members for validation and buy-in. If required, solicit information from PPMT members or other sources as needed.

7.6.2   Validating framework processes with the project portfolio sponsor

The framework decisions need to be validated with the sponsor, and the necessary support secured. In addition, team operating rules need to be clearly understood and confirmed by PPMT members.

7.6.3   Documenting and communicating framework processes

All the decisions arising from the framework are documented for future guidance. The framework document is made available for all PPMT members for reference. Decisions may be altered as the PPMT matures, but buy-in for any proposed changes is required. Finally, consistent application of framework decisions is critical for the success of the portfolio implementation; the PMO manager has a key role to play in enforcing the framework.

CHAPTER 8

Create prioritisation procedures and guidelines

The purpose of this chapter is to suggest how to establish procedures and guidelines for prioritising the organisation's projects. It is intended to provide a starting point from which to establish a project prioritisation process. Prioritisation is the process in which some project work is given preference over other project work, based on specific prioritisation criteria which represent the business strategies.

Typical recommended key steps when engaging in a prioritisation process include:

- defining project domains by creating a project hit-list
- assessing the clarity of project proposals or business cases
- defining prioritisation criteria
- creating or updating the project registry
- prioritising projects

In the prioritisation process, the types of project work must be clearly defined and the list of projects must be comprehensive. The project information provided must be accurate and complete, as decisions are to be made based on the facts and supported by a consistently applied process. A key consideration is that prioritisation decisions need to be consciously aligned with business strategies.

The portfolio management process uses prioritisation to ensure that the projects most likely to implement strategy are allocated the needed resources. The aspect of converting strategy into reality demands that the right resources be allocated to get the work done through projects. As a result, in the prioritisation process it is essential to derive the strategic objectives and determine the criteria which then help rank the projects in order of business importance.

Within organisations, priorities are assessed on a daily basis, as project managers and functional managers are forever involved in decisions regarding which project to work on and for how long. These decisions on resource allocation are based on an assessment of relative priorities. In most cases these priority assessments are made on an ad hoc basis, not in a managed way and not continually to be improved as a controlled process. As prioritisation influences the outcome of business strategies, it is clearly a process associated with the leadership function and not to be delegated.

8.1   Defining project domains by creating a project hit-list

The first step in the prioritisation process is for the PPMT to identify the categories of business opportunities through defined domains or types of work within which funding profiles can be determined. This facilitates the appropriate and efficient allocation of funds to projects in the portfolio without organisationally excluding any type of project. Typically, a project hit-list is created that collects and consolidates standard project information.

8.1.1   Defining the domains of project work

The PPMT analyses the domains that organise the project work into common types, and validates the domains with the portfolio sponsor. This facilitates the comprehensive categorisation of projects for resource, funding, and evaluation purposes.

Project domains can be defined in many different ways, based on the focus of the organisation. A domain can be described as the grouping of projects to which a standard set of criteria can be applied for prioritisation. For example, domains can be classified as products like enterprise systems, personal peripherals, printers or intranet hardware. Other classifications can include service type, industry, geographical area, functional area, or customer type among others. It is strongly recommended that the portfolio process start within a small domain and roll out across the organisation. In the current environment companies that have gone with a 'big bang' deployment have failed miserably.

In most circumstances project domains tend to be based on how the organisation currently structures itself to accomplish its work. This can sometimes be quite straightforward while at other times, domains may not exactly align with the organisational structure. As the domain parameters demand a set of unique characteristics so that projects can be easily defined as belonging to that specific domain, it becomes essential that the domains defined be mutually exclusive.

8.1.2   Allocating budgets to the domains identified

Budget allocation means determining the resource capacity of each domain within the portfolio; it is a critical decision reflecting the business strategy. It is crucial that the PPMT clearly understand the business model used for the appropriate allocation. Poor or unclear allocation can have both short and long term impact on business realities. The basis for resource allocation can be influenced by several factors, such as:

- industry standards
- business history
- politics of the 'squeaky wheel' – the one that makes the loudest noise
- a domain's role definition within the organisation
- availability of resources – people and capital
- cost tracking/accounting systems

The PPMT must ensure that allocation remains within each targeted portfolio level and is consistent with the overall budgetary boundary conditions. At the initial point in the portfolio process the PPMT's level of understanding of the business strategies becomes critical, and the executive management team should be available to clarify strategies in the light of budget allocation concerns. As the portfolio process becomes embedded and matured in the organisation, the measured effectiveness of the process will have profound ramifications for the resource budget allocation process. The organisations we have worked with have often found it beneficial to tie their fiscal budgeting processes to this step in the project portfolio process.

8.1.3   Identifying project proposals by domain

The PPMT must ensure that each project on their hit-list is the subject of a formulated proposal. If such a proposal has not been submitted, the PPMT must see that it is forthcoming. It is important for the PPMT to carry out an initial 'sanity check' for completeness of the proposal. Each proposal must be assigned to a single domain. In the event that the proposal seems to fit within more than one domain, the PPMT needs either to consider re-examining the domains for mutual exclusivity, to place the project in the domain where it has the greatest potential benefits, or to add/define a new domain. On the other hand, if the proposal does not fit any defined domain of the portfolio, then the PPMT needs in addition to consider the option of removing the project from the portfolio.

8.1.4 Defining domain registry parameters

The PPMT must understand the strategies specific to each project domain and recognise the differences in domain priorities. The PPMT must therefore document those domain strategies and priorities. As a minimum requirement the PPMT must establish a project registry within each domain which identifies parameters such as the project size/level of effort; duration of project; significance of business contribution; level of project maturity (life cycle phase), and degree of project definition. However, if a projects falls outside of the registry parameters then the PPMT may need to consider the following options:

- moving to the next cycle
- moving to another domain
- funding with discretionary budgets
- cancelling the project

8.2 Defining prioritisation criteria

Defining the right prioritisation criteria will support and enhance the alignment of project work with the business strategies within the organisation. The criteria provide guidance for the proposals that support PPMT portfolio ranking activities and also define the project ranking model.

8.2.1 Identifying the business strategies

This may be the single most written-about subject in business texts. The PPMT must have a basic understanding of business strategy fundamentals so as to put the portfolio in the proper context and thereby support the development of an effective portfolio management process.

As a strategy is to implement a vision and a project is to implement a strategy, the task of the PPMT is to implement the portfolio process which provides the organisation with the opportunity to tangibly share the experience of attaining the vision. The strategy defines the direction from which actions are measured for their contribution to organisational benefit. Those actions are organised, for effective management, in the form of projects. The strategy is translated into operational results through the application of project work. The portfolio management process ensures the correct allocation of the organisation's resources to those projects offering the greatest contribution toward the strategy.

The greatest challenge faced by PPMT members and even consultants is that of finding out the strategy of the company. How do we discover it? In most cases it tends to be found, whether hidden or explicit, in one or more of these sources:

- annual reports
- vision/mission statements
- capability statements
- corporate history/legend
- corporate behaviour

Upon discovering the strategy the PPMT must document its findings, as this serves to determine the criteria against which to assess projects and their relative value. The organisation's strategy is the most important foundation for the validation of portfolio ranking. There is a potential for misusing the PPM process to reverse-engineer or even adjust the business strategies. Therefore the PPMT must avoid the temptation to redefine the organisation's strategy and maintain the appropriate relationship between strategy and the portfolio management process.

On an ongoing basis, the PPMT must regularly review the portfolio process to ensure alignment with the business strategies. In our current business environment, that demands speed and agility as business strategies are often updated and quickly modified.

8.2.2　Defining strategy related criteria

The PPMT needs to define criteria to represent each of the identified business strategies. A criterion is a standard on which a judgment or decision may be based. The prioritisation criteria establish a tangible relationship between the proposed work and the business strategies of the organisation.

The PPMT must work closely with the portfolio sponsor during this process as this allows for easier validation later on. Each element of the business strategy must correspond with a prioritisation criterion, as shown in Figure 32.

There are many different characteristics of good criteria, including:

Business strategy	Prioritisation criterion
• Expand globally • Be profitable • Maintain our financial position • Leverage success, without leveraging assets	• Market penetration • Return on investment (ROI) • Up-front investment • Uses existing technology

Figure 32 Mapping business strategies onto prioritisation criteria

- few in number
- orthogonal (no overlap)
- understandable
- clearly measurable
- consistently applicable
- linked directly to strategy
- appropriate to portfolio focus and domains

The collective set of prioritisation criteria will be used to assess a proposed project's potential contribution to implementing the business strategies identified. The assessment of proposed project work against a set of prioritisation criteria eliminates the unhealthy competition between projects that occurs when projects are assessed against one another.

As criteria are highly dependent on strategy, the PPMT must understand that differing strategies suggest different criteria. Typically, financial criteria are of ultimate importance for making resource allocation decisions; however, broader strategic, commercial and technical values are significant as well. Typical criteria are shown in Figure 33.

A good criterion, when applied, supports strategy and balances all financial, technical, commercial and strategic concerns. As a result, you need to be mindful of the fact that prioritisation criteria are used to reflect business strategies – not to advance favoured projects. When defining the criteria, make sure that the focus is on equity in the representation of business strategies. A well set criterion allows for differentiation between 'clear winners' and 'obvious losers'. As the business/portfolio environment changes, the criteria need to be adjusted as well – revalidation and resetting of criteria must be accommodated within the Project Portfolio Management process.

The prioritisation criteria may undergo several rounds of reconsideration and validation as the PPMT's understanding of the process grows. The impact and actual meaning of the prioritisation criteria may not be

Intangible ◄─────────────────────────────► Tangible			
Strategic	**Commercial**	**Technical**	**Financial**
Support of core competencies	Clear market need	Complexity of solution	Net present value (NPV)
Synergy with other project efforts	Right market timing	Degree of technical risk	Payback schedule
Consistency with executive leadership vision / business intuition	Improves competitive positioning	Reliability requirements	Internal rate of return (IRR)
Supports corporate reorganisation	Obvious value proposition	Skills development	Return on investment (ROI)
Meets shareholder interests	Gains access to new markets (market penetration)		Development costs
Matches corporate culture			Commercialisation costs
			Cost-to-complete

Figure 33 Project criteria

fully appreciated by the PPMT until the later stage of the portfolio process when the criteria are applied to the scoring models (see section 8.2.5). It is inevitable that as the business atmosphere or portfolio environment changes, the prioritisation criteria will need to be adjusted as well.

8.2.3   Defining proposal content requirements

The PPMT determines and documents the content requirements for the proposals that the organisation submits for project work. This ensures that the proposals received for consideration directly address the prioritisation criteria established for aligning project work with business strategies. Defining proposal content is part of the project portfolio process for these reasons:

- The PPMT evaluates the prioritisation criteria in the light of the type of information needed about projects, in order to measure each project's alignment with business strategies.

- Important evaluation information is identified and communicated to the organisation to ensure that proposals address the criteria used to assess project priority.
- Proposal information is arrived at prior to determining weighting and scoring anchors, in order to avoid placing unnecessary emphasis on any single criterion.
- All proposals should include adequate information to allow the PPMT to make an assessment against the prioritisation criteria.
- Determination of proposal content should be independent of weighting and scoring model decisions, thus allowing those decisions to change without constantly changing proposal content requirements.

Based on the need to assess projects using the defined prioritisation criteria, the PPMT should determine what information is required about the projects within each domain. In many ways each domain may have its own unique informational requirements and the project information submitted to the PPMT should support the meeting of the relevant criterion.

The PPM process interfaces with the organisational proposal process – it does not replace it. At the initial stage of the implementation, the proposal content requirements may need to be adjusted once some typical project proposals have been submitted to the PPMT – this allows for the valuable benefits of self-correcting iteration. Although the PPMT needs good information to effectively conduct the portfolio process, one must be careful not to place too many demands on the proposal process; if proposals are too difficult to prepare, project teams will attempt to proceed without them. As the PPMT gains more experience in applying the criteria using the project proposal information, the proposal content requirement may need to be refined.

8.2.4 Establishing weighted values of the criteria

The PPMT evaluates each criterion in relation to the other criteria and establishes a weighted value of each, indicating the relative significance of each criterion. This facilitates the selection of project work as it more closely relates to the significant business strategies of the organisation. The weight is defined as an assigned multiplier associated with each criterion for the purpose of quantifying the relationship between the various criteria.

In determining the relative value of criteria, the PPMT needs to consider that the criteria are not all equal, and that they are to be driven by organisational needs. In addition, a cross-functional perspective is important in the valuation of the criteria. As a ranking will be given to projects based on the criteria, it is essential that these are well understood by all so as to create buy-in of PPMT assessment and project ranking. In most companies, the criteria are typically developed by the portfolio manager and validated by the PPMT.

The following list provides a simple guideline on the considerations to be taken into account when establishing weights for each criterion:

- Each criterion is evaluated against other criteria.
- Weight is assigned independent of project considerations.
- Simple is better – do not argue over minor differences in scale. For example, weights of 0.5, 1.0, and 1.5 (below norm, norm, above norm) are easier to assign than using a 1-to-10 scale.
- Weighting is not an exercise in how much more important one criterion is than another; rather it is an exercise in identifying their relative strategic or business emphasis.
- Weighting of criteria may change as the strategic intent of the organisation changes.
- The key objective is to create a system that promotes clear separation between top priority projects and lower priority projects within the portfolio/domain.
- Weights are likely to differ between domains even if they happen to share the same prioritisation criteria, due to a difference in the strategic emphasis of the various domains.

When the weighted value of each criterion has been determined by the PPMT, it is then documented and validated by the portfolio sponsor before transferral to the project registry. As mentioned, the application of the agreed weighting will benefit from the iterative, self-correcting characteristics of the PPM process. The PPMT needs to experiment with the weighting factors to determine their appropriateness within the project portfolio. The PPM framework should address the need for regular review of the criteria and their weighting, so as to ensure that conscious alignment with business strategies is maintained

8.2.5 Defining the project scoring model

The PPMT determines the process and measurement scale that will be used to assess proposed and ongoing project work against each criterion. This ensures that the PPMT members understand and concur on the valuation for each criterion. A *scoring model* is the system of rules and practices used to apply the prioritisation criteria to all projects within a specific domain. A *scoring anchor* is the written description of the measurement applied to the numeric value of the scoring model.

The PPMT should work as a team in a collaborative manner to develop the scoring model(s). There are many different methods for using weighted criteria to 'score' projects. However, the important consideration for establishing the scoring model is to make sure that the results are clearly understood. A word of caution is needed concerning the use of complex models, which usually result in questions about scoring validity; if the model is complex and the results are not easily understood, then the tendency is to question the quality of the priority assessment. It is strongly recommended that a simple matrix structure, with multiplied scoring based on criteria weights, meets most needs.

The weighted totals are tabulated for each project in the domain. The project score on each prioritisation criterion (1 to 5) is multiplied by the prioritisation criterion weight (0.5, 1.0, 1.5). It is best to adapt the scoring model so that it best meets the portfolio/domain needs. An example of the scoring model is shown in Figure 34.

Here are some basic rules to follow when developing the scoring model:

- Use anchors to promote easy assessment of projects.
- Make sure each anchor is a clear, unambiguous definition of how the score is to be applied.
- The model should provides a reference point for PPMT scoring deliberations.
- Make the ranking scale small; 1 to 5 is recommended.
- Rate each project completely before moving on to the next project.
- Compute the total scores.

↗ **Establish weighted values for the prioritisation criteria:**

Market penetration	ROI	Up-front investment	Uses existing technology
(1.5)	(1.0)	(0.5)	(1.0)

↗ **Define scoring anchors:**

Market penetration	ROI	Up-front investment	Uses existing technology
1 = No new markets 3 = Growth in existing markets 5 = Intro to target market(s)	1 = Negative ROI 3 = Breakeven 5 = Positive ROI	1 = Exceeds current budget 3 = Within current budget 5 = None required	1 = Difficult to acquire 3 = Easily acquired 5 = No new technology

Figure 34 Creating a portfolio scoring model

Each domain will have its own scoring model and it is recommended to evaluate each scoring model individually to ensure that:

- each model reflects the domain's role within the business strategies
- the prioritisation criteria are clearly understood
- each prioritisation criterion is appropriately weighted for the domain
- the rating scale is defined
- clear scaling anchors are set to provide meaning to the ratings

The PPMT should document the scoring model process to promote consistency. Training and education on the scoring model and process are required for PPMT members, PMO staff and the appropriate project and portfolio sponsors.

It is important to recognise the iterative, self-correcting nature of this process and allow for the iteration to take place. The scoring models need to be adjusted and refined based on how effectively they serve the process once projects are actually scored against them.

Although the scoring models may be adjusted throughout the application of the PPM process, consistent operation of the scoring process is extremely important. This is best achieved through a well defined and clearly documented scoring model and the work of a disciplined team that applies the process consistently and effectively.

8.3   Creating or updating the project registry

All proposed and in-process project work is identified, reviewed for thoroughness of documentation and posted to the project registry. This becomes the inventory of project work and the central point for the documentation and communication of project status. The PPMT will need to ensure that the portfolio is up to date and complete before scoring projects. In addition, the PPMT needs to validate the accuracy of the proposal information and if required ask project managers to formally submit proposals to the PPMT for consideration.

8.3.1   Performing a 'sanity check' on submitted proposals

The PPMT initially reviews each proposal and assigns it to the appropriate domain within the project portfolio. This ensures that the proposals are evaluated for possible approval against the appropriate prioritisation criteria.

One of the challenges for the PPMT is to determine what is to count as a project. It is important to validate the organisation's current parameters for defining a project as documented in the framework processes. A project is a unique effort with a defined beginning, a defined end, a specific deliverable, and defined resource requirements. The gathering of project information is a mechanical task; however, the best source of project information are the proposals written with the project portfolio content requirements as guidance – and such proposals may not be readily available.

The top-down view of the work going on in an organisation needs bottom-up validation. The PPMT needs to survey the organisation and compile a comprehensive list of work going on within the organisation. In the survey process there need to be clear definitions of project work and non-project work. Companies are often surprised to find out how much project work is in fact going on, and also shocked to find out how much previously unidentified work is using resources but does not qualify under the above definition of a project.

In identifying project work it commonly occurs that certain projects are forgotten, such as investigation activities, customer management and support, documenting existing processes, process improvement activities, minor product enhancements/customisations and project proposal activities; and so-called 'skunk works'.

On the other hand, while identifying non-project work there is a tendency to forget tasks like meetings, administrative work, bug fixes, customer management, interviewing and hiring, training and pre-project research.

It is as well to remember that non-project work is not of lesser value to the organisation than project work – but it is managed differently. In addition, information about the amount of non-project work is required to determine true resource availability. In organisations, resource availability is often overstated because it does not account for the amount and type of non-project work. Figure 35 shows, among other things, that at least two to three times as many projects exist as compared to the perception of the management. Furthermore there is a mismatch of actual resource available for project work. This funnelling occurs as a result of ambiguity in the definitions of project and non-project work.

The PPMT reviews each proposal for thoroughness of content and usefulness of information for evaluation purposes. This facilitates the prompt and efficient evaluation of the proposal and assures consistency of decisions made regarding project approval or status. Project proposal status, based on the 'sanity check', can be either:

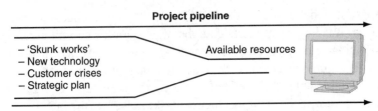

Project pipeline

- 'Skunk works'   Available resources
- New technology
- Customer crises
- Strategic plan

- At least 2–3 times more projects than perceived by management
- No more than 50% (and usually less) of expected resources actually available
- Executives fight fires and individual contributors choose their own work, defocusing objectives

Figure 35 Project portfolio mismatch due to ambiguous definition of work

- acceptance for consideration/scoring; or
- conditional acceptance, pending required changes; or
- reconsideration at a later time; or
- rejection.

Project registry 'gatekeeping' responsibility is critical to the effectiveness of the PPMT. The 'sanity check' does not authorise a project to proceed, but only means that it is adjudged to be at an acceptable level of quality for PPMT consideration.

The 'sanity check' or quality review should be viewed as an opportunity to educate the project environment as to the information required for the PPMT to make the right decisions. As the PPM process matures and the project 'community' becomes more aware of the proposal quality requirement, the quality of proposals should improve. The proposals that consistently 'miss the mark' during the quality review should be used to improve the proposal process. In addition, the quality review of project proposals should be indicative of the effectiveness of communicating the proposal requirements and the prioritisation criteria on which they are based.

8.3.2   Adding proposed projects to the registry

All newly proposed projects that have passed a quality review are entered into the project registry. This facilitates both communication within the organisation, and evaluation of proposed projects in relation to ongoing projects. A project registry is the complete and accurate list of accepted projects and proposed projects within the portfolio. Minimum information requirements for the project registry include:

- project sponsor name
- project manager name
- project priority ranking
- target milestone schedule
- resource requirements
- identified domain within the project portfolio

The PPMT should assess the project registry needs and select the best tool to support the PPM process. The registry needs to make use of an automated database.

It is critically important to maintain process integrity and to ensure that all projects follow the proposal submittal and registration processes. Any shortcuts to portfolio registration devalue the process, as project proponents may perceive that some projects get 'special treatment'. In certain circumstances the PPMT may consider 'fast-track' processing to allow for time-sensitive efforts, but a word of caution is in order: exceptions are likely to become the norm.

The first time the project registry is completed all projects will have 'acceptance for consideration/scoring' status because they have not yet been prioritised. When the project registry is initiated, include all projects under way in the organisation, regardless of where they are in the project life cycle.

During implementation of the PPM process the project registry should be agreed to by functional managers and made available to them, to ensure a common understanding of resource availability. This helps to avoid the problem of understating or overstating resource availability.

Functional managers should have regular access to the project registry to ensure that the understanding of project work in the organisation is consistent with the resource availability posted in the project registry.

8.3.3   Submitting proposals to the PPMT for consideration

Projects that have 'acceptance for consideration/scoring' status in the project registry are added to the agenda of the next suitable PPMT meeting. This provides assurances to the PPMT that the proposed project work which they review is consistent with established standards and can be reliably evaluated alongside other project work in the organisation. The PMO provides the PPMT with the updated project registry and the necessary project information to ensure the PPMT has everything it needs to correctly score the proposed projects against the domain prioritisation criteria.

PPMT members should receive the information on proposed projects prior to the scoring activity to allow for necessary preparation. The PPMT member from the organisational area that created the project proposal should be prepared to represent the proposal to the PPMT and resolve outstanding issues with the proposal team. In some circumstances, the PPMT leader can assign a member of the PPMT to be the proposal advocate if there is not an obvious organisational advocate on the PPMT.

The relationship and division of responsibilities between the PPMT and the PMO will take some time to be clearly understood. The effective conduct of this step may be impacted by the personalities of the team members involved, and as membership turnover occurs, the processes should be revalidated. In some cases, the PPMT member serving as an advocate for an organisational area may not support the proposed project; however, their role is to serve as an advocate for the area, not as a proposal screen. Finally, all projects that meet the domain parameters and pass the proposal quality review standards are considered by the PPMT for prioritisation.

8.3.4 Updating the registry with project status information

Prior to evaluating newly proposed project work, the PPMT also receives status information on the ongoing project work of the organisation. This ensures that all project work is evaluated in its most current state and that the consequences of the decisions made are relevant to the current status of the work.

Project status information varies during the different phases of project maturity; project managers are responsible for updating status information in the registry. The registry should include an historical listing of project status for each project. The PMO needs to bear in mind that it is their responsibility to ensure that the necessary updated information is available in the registry so that the PPMT can be effective in discharging its duties.

Project managers may need to be encouraged to provide updated project status information on a regular basis, and it is important for the PMO to demonstrate to project managers the benefit of regularly providing updated information to the registry.

8.4 Prioritising projects

Newly proposed project work is evaluated alongside the ongoing project work of the organisation; a determination must be made as to the priority ranking of proposed and ongoing projects. This evaluation, using the weighted prioritisation criteria and the corresponding scoring models, ensures that project work and the associated resource assignments are prioritised to secure alignment with the business strategies of the organisation.

8.4.1   Scoring proposed projects using the scoring model

Newly proposed projects are evaluated using the scoring model previously determined for each domain. This ensures that all project work is evaluated by the same standards and is given equal consideration. The scoring model must be applied consistently to each project in the updated registry, with projects being rated against the prioritisation criteria and not against each other. The PPMT must conduct the scoring collaboratively; that is, as a team, not with each member scoring individually and then the results being consolidated. This creates the opportunity for cross-functional consideration of projects, and minimises the possibility of function based concerns or preferences. In addition, collaborative scoring avoids the preservation of resources for those 'pet' projects which would not otherwise be scored high.

When applying the scoring models, the emphasis is placed on meeting the prioritisation criteria in support of the business strategies, with projects evaluated on the basis of their contribution to those strategies. Scoring on this basis de-emphasises the competitive aspect of project comparison. Best practice is to score on a project-by-project basis, that is, with each single project scored against the full set of prioritisation criteria, then the next project, and so on until the full set of projects within the domain has been scored. It is strongly recommended that projects are not scored on a prioritisation criterion-by-criterion basis, as this approach only serves to encourage competition between projects by attempting to rank-order the projects against each criterion. Examples of scores entered into the scoring model are shown in Figure 36.

	Market penetration (1.5)	ROI (1.0)	Up-front investment (0.5)	Uses existing technology (1.0)	Total score
Invention	1	3	2	1	6.5
Enter Asia	5	5	1	3	16.0
Firewall	1	5	3	1	9.0
Upgrader	1	4	1	5	11.0
Revamp	1	3	5	4	11.0
Innovation	3	5	5	3	15.0
Automator	2	5	3	3	12.5

Figure 36 Scoring projects (example)

The scoring process promotes dynamic decision making. Transferral of updated scores into a software application is not complicated.

The PPMT leader should facilitate the scoring process to accomplish two important goals: a content goal and a process goal. The content goal is to score the projects within the portfolio for prioritisation; the process goal is to promote active debate/discussion among PPMT members. Perhaps the biggest benefit of the scoring model is the interactive discussion and dynamic decision making of the PPMT membership. Other values gained as a result of the project scoring process are:

- The appropriate balance of functional concerns and strategic objectives is realised.
- The reliability of existing measurements of business success and the recognition of better measures are acknowledged.
- The emphasis on one business strategy over another is often debated.
- The quality of the proposal development process can be reassessed when unexpected scores emerge.

In the early stages of PPM implementation the prioritisation criteria are likely to be questioned by the PPMT in terms of their definition and validity. This is to be anticipated; as the PPMT progresses, it learns to apply the scoring model, and repeated clarifying of the prioritisation criteria, ranking scale and anchors will help maintain the PPMT's focus.

Important and challenging questions, reaching far beyond preparation for allocating resources, often arise from the results of project scoring and must be addressed. The PPMT will need some time to absorb the impact of these discussions. On an ongoing basis it is normal for the PPMT to want to adjust and refine the scoring model nearly every time it is applied; however, be sure that the adjustments are made for the right reasons.

8.4.2 Ranking projects

In this step, the PPMT places the proposed and ongoing project work in descending order according to the results of the scoring models. Based on this order ranking, an implied priority is established. This facilitates optimisation of available resources.

Projects are placed in numerical order based on the total score determined by applying the scoring model. At this stage resource concerns are not considered. The rank order is first determined by the scoring model as a basis for the PPMT's discussion of rank-order appropriateness. Next,

		Market penetration (1.5)	ROI (1.0)	Up-front investment (0.5)	Uses existing technology (1.0)	Total score
1	Enter Asia	5	5	1	3	16.0
2	Innovation	3	5	5	3	15.0
3	Automator	2	5	3	3	12.5
4	Upgrader	1	4	1	5	11.0
5	Revamp	1	3	5	4	11.0
6	Firewall	1	5	3	1	9.0
7	Invention	1	3	2	1	6.5

Figure 37 Ranking projects (example)

based on the ranking, the PPMT can assign initial priorities to each project by domain.

It is important to keep the scoring process in its proper context; for example, do not lose sight of the fact that the scoring process is simply a tool, which cannot replace good decision making. It is also likely that a healthy scepticism about the scoring process will arise, and indeed should be encouraged by the PPMT leader. Examples of scores entered in rank order are shown in Figure 37.

Once the initial priorities have been set by the scoring process, the PPMT should evaluate the rank order and the corresponding priorities from a common sense and business perspective. It is typical for the PPMT members to have preconceived expectations about project ranking based on their own inherent sense of priorities, but project prioritisation arrived at by the process described here will most often not match those expectations.

If there are any initial project priorities that intuitively challenge a PPMT member's views, the PPMT should identify the issue, attempt to locate the root cause of the questioned priority, and highlight the concern for consideration and resolution during the 'balancing the resources' and project selection stages of the PPM process.

Just like the previous process of scoring projects, prioritisation is a simple mechanical step that may nevertheless have rather large implications for the management of the organisation. Managing the project ranking activity to accomplish both the content goal (prioritisation) and the process goal (discussing the ramifications of the priorities) is an important role for the PPMT leader.

Normally key business issues come up as a result of project prioritisation, including:

- testing of the soundness of current business strategies, and identification of missing strategic aims that have somehow been overlooked
- questioning of the validity of previously used management decision making processes, and recognition of the underlying reasons for their success or failure
- examination of the appropriateness of the organisational structure for managing project work

It will be a challenge for the PPMT, in the initial stages of the process, to create the right balance, while using the scoring process with discipline and questioning the outcomes based on business intuition. Yet with experience the PPMT will become more accustomed to the scoring/prioritisation process. As a way to improve the outcome, make sure that the questions about prioritisation lead to an active search to find the root cause of the questions, and make appropriate adjustments to the scoring process.

It is to be expected that some important projects may just not score well and initially receive low priority; however, the results should be open to question, making sure that the 'why' question is always considered first.

8.4.3 Validate priority rankings with the portfolio sponsor

The PPMT leader and portfolio sponsor must review the outcome of the priority rankings. This provides an opportunity for the PPMT leader and the portfolio sponsor to consider the priorities and recommend optimisation tactics.

Although many decisions about the process for prioritising the portfolio will previously have been validated, the impact of those decisions is best evidenced in the project prioritisation itself – this may motivate the sponsor to revalidate. For example, key decisions which were previously validated may be reopened and require further validation, such as:

- how the business strategies are to be understood by the PPMT
- the selection of prioritisation criteria to represent those business strategies
- the relative importance attached to the business strategies, as expressed through the prioritisation criteria weighting
- the project information needed, as articulated in the proposal content requirements

CHAPTER 9

Map resource capacity and demand

In organisations the resource capacity is pulled from all sides by project demand. The resource capacity is defined as the organisation's facility or power to produce or deploy resources for project work. The resource demand is the quantity and skill requirements of resources needed for project work at a specified time.

Resource decisions are plagued with difficult challenges. In most organisations there are too many projects and not enough resources, together with mismatches of skill-sets. Another common pitfall is that of the organisation treating availability as a skill-set. Other problems in resource management include:

- valuable resource being expended on non-valuable projects
- a 'use it or lose it' philosophy
- reserving resources based on functional 'ownership', without regard for organisational requirements
- poor resource demand estimation practices such as padding and poor negotiation; and undue optimism or pessimism about resource availability
- giving 80 per cent of the attention to 20 per cent of the problems (the Pareto principle)

Before deciding what to do, collect and understand the facts. This means conducting a resource assessment. Typically a resource assessment is characterised by the following activities:

- distinguishing the resource skill-sets
- identifying the truly necessary resources
- qualifying key project assumptions
- efficiently managing the resource information
- continuous updating of resource capacity data
- validating true resource demands
- building organisational commitment to resource assignments

- establishing consistent and reliable resource requirement estimation practices
- interactively prioritising projects and resource requirements
- identifying resource capacity versus resource demand issues
- documenting budget decisions

Functional managers identify the availability and skill-sets of staff for project work and ensure that this data is entered into the supporting software. This represents the 'supply' side of the 'supply and demand' equation as the PPMT reconciles project resource demands with available resources. All management decisions are indicative of true organisational commitment to business strategy and resource commitments are the tangible evidence of the decision process.

9.1　Defining the resource pool

The purpose of defining the resource pool is to document the functional levels (organisational breakdown structure or OBS) that will be used to identify and appropriately assign resources to proposed project work, including skill-sets, special abilities and the personnel. This facilitates a common organisational approach to accounting for resource availability and skills.

9.1.1　Defining the organisational breakdown structure (OBS)

In mapping the resource structure of an organisation, the OBS begins with functional mapping and ends with the identification of skill-sets at the appropriate level of granularity. It is important to examine how the organisation structures its resources for project work per project portfolio. Typically the OBS closely parallels the existing organisational structure until it gets to a skill-sets level of detail. This can be presented as an organisational chart, as shown in Figure 38.

Functional managers should work closely with the PMO manager to ensure that the needs of functional areas and of the PPMT are met. The level of detail in the OBS depends on portfolio and domain concerns. The essential minimum level of detail recommended is one that can capture skill-sets such as those needed by software engineers, testing lab staff, customer representatives and so on. It may even be necessary to include special abilities in the OBS, like those of C++ programmer, test script writer, hydraulics installer, and financial expert among others.

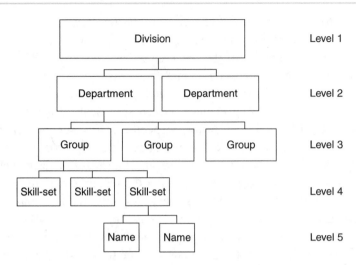

Figure 38 Building the organisational breakdown structure

It is strongly recommended to include specific names in the OBS chart. In preparing the chart, consider the benefits and tradeoffs when deciding what level of detail is to be included.

A resource pool can be defined as a group of people available to accomplish project work within the project portfolio – a 'resource' for portfolio management can also include non-human resources that are distinctive or scarce, for example test labs, research equipment and so on.

In identifying project resources, determine the percentage of time allocated directly to project work by any person who works on projects, which can include full-time and part-time project team members. The person (resource) assigned to the portfolio must be identified by name and matching skills. It is important to include all persons (resources) who contribute directly to project work, whether or not their time is 100 per cent committed to project work. It is also important to bear in mind that functional managers may be contributing resources to more than one project domain. As a result, functional managers must work closely with the PMO manager to ensure a common understanding of the resource capacity of any given group of projects. In situations where a particular person (resource) performs project work for multiple domains within the portfolio, that person is assigned to a 'host' domain. It is the responsibility of the functional manager to proactively seek resolution of any questions that arise regarding the appropriate allocation of a person (resource) to a specific project domain.

The OBS and the resource pool may be developed simultaneously, but it is essential that they be compared and contrasted with each other to check for inconsistencies. The OBS is the top-down look at project resources; an inventory of project team members is a bottom-up look at those resources. Analysis of the resource pool against the OBS helps to identify any mismatch between people and skills.

Refinement of the OBS and the resource pool should be carried out in an iterative, self-correcting manner. Watch specifically for members of the resource pool who do not fit into a specified OBS category and highlight any OBS categories that do not have any specific persons (resources) assigned to them. Functional managers and the PMO manager need to work jointly in comparing and contrasting the resource requirements.

In the initial implementation of the PPM process there may be lot of inconsistencies and missing resources as between the OBS and the resource pool. A word of caution: do not define the OBS at too low a level of detail, as the PPM process is not designed to be used for managing the day-to-day task activities of every person (resource) in the entire organisation.

In some cases, functional managers may be less than forthcoming in providing full data about resources. This may be due to a mistaken feeling of losing control. It is the responsibility of the PPMT to make it clear that the benefits of the process are shared by the individual functions as well as the entire portfolio community.

As the PPM process becomes more embedded within the organisation, refinement of the OBS and resource pool becomes an ongoing activity; and as the process demonstrates its effectiveness, functional organisations will want to increase the number of persons (resources) that are taken into consideration as part of the process.

9.1.2 Quantifying the resources available for project work

Functional managers determine the availability of each person specifically for project work. This provides the PPMT with a realistic view of resource availability and assists in avoiding overallocation of resources.

It is quite common to use the term 'full-time equivalent' (FTE) to represent the number of available resource hours, divided by a typical eight-hour work day, needed to complete a task. For example, three people working half-time (12 available hours per day) represent 1.5 FTEs (12 hours / 8 hours per day = 1.5). It is important to have information on all direct project work, that is, work being performed that expressly contributes to the advancement of specific tasks within a project plan.

Use the OBS and resource pool to determine resource availability for project work. However, in arriving at the real resource availability the PPMT must understand the effects of multi-tasking and time contention. In addition, the impact of project and non-project work on availability must be considered with a degree of caution, to temper undue 'resource optimism'.

Functional managers and the PPMT must work collaboratively to ensure that their understanding of project versus non-project work is consistent with the definition of project work as documented in the framework. Identify the percentage of time each person (resource) is contributing to direct project work. For example, project status meetings are not 'direct project work' unless the meetings have been included as tasks in the project plan. Another situation is that updates of information that are routinely shared between various project team members are not 'direct project work' unless time has specifically been allocated to such communication in the project plan.

There are different ways of quantifying the availability of all project resources. For example, if the OBS is crafted to the detail level of specified names, each person's availability should be expressed in the percentage of each work day they have available for direct project work (example: the availability of a person assigned half-time to direct project work would be expressed as '0.5'). However, if the OBS is not crafted to the detail level of specified names, resource availability for direct project work should be expressed in FTEs for the full group of applicable personnel (example: five people assigned half-time to direct project work represents 2.5 FTEs).

Resource availability variation is inevitable. Some organisations are susceptible to seasonal or cyclical fluctuations in the amount of non-project work. A high-growth business environment will be likely to experience increases in non-project work at a more rapid pace than project work. The PMO, working with the PPMT, will need to establish framework processes that can promote continual monitoring and updating of the OBS, the resource pool, and the resource availability for project work as reported by functional managers.

9.1.3 Updating the resource management tool

Resource availability data is entered into the supporting software tool and made available to the PPMT. Entering this data into a common repository encourages organisational behaviour that facilitates the efficient authorisation of resources for project work. A resource management database is designed to allow for the input, consolidation and analysis of resource data. Resource management is the most tedious but significant part of the PPM process, with a lot of data to be managed and with many interdependencies. As a result, using an automated tool can make life easier for everyone.

The resource management software functionality should allow for entry of data at the functional and project levels, with the ability to consolidate at various ascending levels to facilitate programme and portfolio analysis. In addition, resource management functionality should support the optimisation process; permitting 'what if' analysis of resource data.

Non-project work may be tracked in a workforce management database. Resource availability for project work would need to be extracted from the existing software to support the PPM process.

On an ongoing basis the PPMT needs to be ever vigilant in seeing that the emphasis on providing updates to the tool does not overwhelm the emphasis on the PPM process itself, which is where the focus must remain.

9.2   Estimating resource demand

The required resources for completing the organisation's project work are validated and gathered for consideration against resource availability and skill-sets. In estimating resource demand, the PPMT needs to follow four steps:

1   extracting project information and resource demand from project plans
2   validating project information and resource demand with project sponsors
3   updating the project registry
4   performing preliminary analysis of resource capacity and demand

9.2.1   Extracting project information and resource demand from project plans

The resource demands, skill-set requirements and target milestone schedule are collected for proposed and ongoing project work. This gives the PPMT the necessary information to ensure accurate consideration of resource demands.

Project managers extract their initial resource demand estimates from their project plan and other project documents and make sure the resource demand information meets with PPMT requirements. Typical PPMT resource information requirements can include:

- type of resource information – people and capital expenses
- specific format of information – bar charts, histograms, pie charts, and so on
- level of detail – summary of skill-sets versus specific personnel
- length of resource forecast – near term or long term
- key assumptions and supporting data expected

Key resource assumptions and expectations are documented for further review. Project managers need to examine the resource information submitted and identify any potential issues, such as:

- requirements for skills that are not evident in the existing organisation
- skills requirements that are unique and traditionally overdemanded in the organisation
- work in the current project proposal that is a reworking of previous projects, which could affect the specific assignment of resources
- resource co-location issues
- team development requirements

At times, project managers need to review and resolve resource requirement issues or inconsistencies with their project teams and project sponsor. In situations where resource issues cannot be resolved within the project team, they should be escalated to the PPMT through the project sponsor.

This is not the time for securing specific resource commitments, since the actual prioritisation of the proposed project has not been melded into the overall portfolio prioritisation. Any additional project parameters, where available, such as scope constraints or schedule concerns, can be considered and highlighted during this part of the process.

In the beginning the PPMT tends to be unsure about what resource information it needs and as a result the tendency will be to request much more information and at a much greater level of detail than is really needed. This is quite normal, but the PPMT must be careful not to overwhelm project managers with its requests. The way forward is for the PPMT to assist and guide the work in partnership with project managers in relation to resource information needs, so as to ensure the effective review of project-specific demand requirements.

9.2.2   Validating project information and resource demand with project sponsor(s)

The project information extracted is reviewed and validated by project sponsors to ensure that it is accurate and in accordance with their views. This ensures the accuracy of the information and confirms management's commitment to the project work. See Figure 39.

Resource demands of projects within the portfolio are the subject of this cycle of validation between project managers and project sponsors. This is also the final opportunity for project managers and project sponsors to ensure that the information best represents their projects prior to resource authorisation. The project manager's primary objective in this validation is to make sure that the resource information is accurate. This validation with the project sponsor also ensures the sponsor's buy-in and commitment.

9.2.3   Updating the project registry

The validated project resource information is entered into the project registry. This facilitates the reconciling of resource demand with capacity. Entry work for resource demand is done at the project level. Consolidation of all project work in the organisation does not occur at this point in the process, as it is specifically called for later on. Project managers must ensure that the project registry accurately reflects resource demands.

Typically, in the beginning the PMO manager will manage the entry work into the project registry; however, it is recommended that project managers also be trained to do so, following an appropriate schedule. Project managers may, at first, view project registry updating as a task

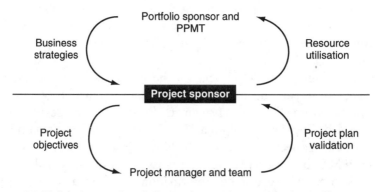

Figure 39 Validating project information and resource demand

they would rather not perform, as they may see little in it by way of added value. The PPMT and the PMO need to stress to project managers the benefits of accurate information and the consequences of PPM process decisions made without the facts. Some PPM software can integrate project plan resource requirements into the project registry relatively easily. This can help project managers to focus on the accuracy of the resource data rather than on managing the entry work.

Updating the project registry with the latest information will quickly demonstrate its value to project managers. It is important to make sure that the PPM process does not undermine the project sponsor's authority and elevate itself above project managers' responsibility to keep their project sponsors informed of project status.

9.2.4 Performing preliminary analysis of resource capacity and demand

The resource capacity and demand information are consolidated at the portfolio level and the PMO performs a preliminary analysis. This provides the PPMT with an initial list of resource considerations, which facilitates the balancing or optimising of the utilisation of resources.

The PMO consolidates the resource capacity information provided by the various functional areas and the resource demand information provided by project managers. This creates a single database, sometimes called a single version of the truth, which facilitates the analysis of resource utilisation.

Let the project registry and resource management software do their jobs – consolidation is easy if wise decisions about the software are made. The consolidated information must be on a regularly scheduled basis. In the beginning the PMO may struggle as it learns its role in the Project Portfolio Management process, particularly as the resource is consolidated and problems are identified. The initial collection and consolidation of resource information is important, so make sure that ample time is allocated to accomplish this work.

There is a danger for the PMO to be tempted to make what it considers to be 'easy fixes' to resource requirement conflicts, which may be outside its scope of authority, resulting in 'premature optimisation' during this time. It is the PPMT who must perform the optimisation or the balancing of the resources with projects as they have the 'big picture' within the organisation.

The PMO manager analyses the consolidated resource capacity and resource demand information and provides the PPMT with a list of resource utilisation issues. This helps to focus the PPMT on the resource issues and facilitates a fact based decision making process during the optimisation stage of the Project Portfolio Management process. The consolidation results must be in a format such that it is easy for the PPMT to identify resource utilisation issues and their impact on the strategic direction of the project portfolio.

The focus of this preliminary review is the identification of issues and considerations that have arisen in the utilisation of resources, given the latest project demand and resource availability updates. Clear utilisation problems are documented on a list and provided to the PPMT to consider during the next PPMT optimisation exercise. There will be some subtleties in the information provided by the database tool that the PMO may not understand until some valuable experience has been gained.

As the organisation gains more experience the obvious utilisation issues will be more quickly identified by those involved in earlier stages of data analysis. Issues that were not previously identified until the PPMT had reviewed the data will be caught by the PMO and eventually by the project manager as they enter the resource information. The ability to review the project resource information at various levels of the project organisation is one of the strengths of the Project Portfolio Management process.

CHAPTER 10

Optimise and balance the project portfolio

Optimisation is the tactical step of balancing resource requirements with resource demand and ensuring that authorised project work is specifically linked to the strategic goals of the organisation. The result of the optimisation process is a prioritised list of projects, with authorised assignment of resources to specific project work. The primary focus is on consciously aligning project work with business strategies using fact based information and good business sense. The ultimate goal is to accomplish the business strategies.

Other objectives of optimisation can include:

- communication of project priorities to the project organisation
- effective utilisation of resources
- predictability in the process, which engenders confidence in the project organisation and focus on optimum results
- balancing of project work, project results, and resource satisfaction

Optimisation is the most critical value-added element of the PPM process. All the previous activities have been designed to prepare for the fact based and often difficult decisions that need to be made during optimisation. The quality of these difficult decisions strongly depends on adherence to the PPM process, which is designed to produce factual information and facilitate fact based decision making. Good, reliable information is needed for optimisation to be successful. Optimisation is based on:

- clear and conscious alignment of project work to business strategies
- comprehensive understanding of the organisation's capacity to make the project work happen
- accurate estimation of required project resources
- knowledge of key decision factors and underlying assumptions
- predictive and consistent project planning and managing processes

In optimisation there is no formulaic decision process; the best information will not guarantee the right outcomes. These attributes are required on the part of the PPMT and others involved in optimisation decisions:

- ability to recognise their immediate functional or project concerns within the grander context of the business strategies of the organisation
- understanding of the interdependencies of project work and the changing nature of project status information
- wisdom in understanding the long term impact of decisions they make today
- power of influencing the organisation to put their decisions into an operational plan

PPMT members must personally take on the responsibilities associated with optimisation – they are tremendously important, and cannot be delegated. Key PPMT responsibilities during the optimisation stage are those of:

- assessing project portfolio information to balance project priorities, resource capacity, and resource demand in support of business strategies
- providing a consistent framework structure for evaluating resource estimates
- documenting the assumptions behind optimisation decisions
- overcoming single-focus functional concerns, while maintaining a global portfolio perspective
- authorising resources for those projects that most effectively contribute to business strategies
- facing up to the difficult decisions
- enforcing the decisions made
- ensuring that the organisation is getting a consistent message from the various PPMT members

10.1 Balancing resource requirements

The PPMT reconciles project resource demands with the organisation's resource capacity. This facilitates the authorisation of resource assignment to priority projects.

10.1.1   Consolidating and reviewing the project registry

A quality review for consistency and viability is performed on the preliminary analysis of resource capacity and demand. This will ensure that the PPMT is reviewing accurate and consistent information.

Updating of resource availability by functional managers is an ongoing effort and is not event driven. Updating of resource demands by project managers is based on the detailed project plans. The focus for this quality review is on resource demands, as functional managers will be continually updating the resource management software with changes in resource capacity.

In the initial stages the PMO's primary task will centre on making sure project managers have input their resource estimates in a timely manner. They also may want to remind functional managers of their responsibility to provide updates to resource capacity information, until it becomes habitual for them. The PMO should also support project managers and functional managers in the practice of an incremental update of the project registry with changes in resource information, which is more effective and easier in the long run that waiting for major changes to accumulate before updating.

On an ongoing basis it is important to the PPM process that quality review results are fed back to the project managers who have entered resource information. The PMO should not place itself in a role of fixing errors for the project managers as a routine practice. Project managers must remain accountable for their resource data entry.

10.1.2   Comparing resource capacity with resource demand

The PPMT reviews the requested resources for project work and compares them with the organisation's resource capacity. This provides an opportunity for the PPMT to ongoingly resolve issues and understand the state of the organisation's resource utilisation. The PPMT identifies resource utilisation issues and their impact on the strategic direction of the project portfolio. The focus of this comparison is that of identifying issues and considerations that have arisen in the utilisation of resources, given the latest project resource demand updates from the planning information submitted by project managers.

10.1.3 Analysing and recommending available options for resource utilisation

The PPMT analyses the overall portfolio and makes recommendations for optimal use of available resources. This facilitates the approval of resource utilisation by management.

Shortfall identification on its own is not enough; root-cause reasons must be understood. The PPMT must engage in 'what if' scenario modelling. There are several portfolio management tools that can be used to perform such modelling, so as to give a clear understanding of the situation if the PPMT were to shift resources.

Some of the scenarios that can be experimented with include:

- delaying lower-priority projects
- cancelling lower-priority projects that have already begun
- delaying particular development phases of a project
- assigning different people (resources) to a project
- splitting the capacity of individual persons (resources) between two or more projects
- hiring temporary contract labour
- reducing non-project work

The PPMT will need some guidance and training to learn to appreciate the information 'behind the numbers'. Make sure that the PPMT does not bury itself in the analysis of the information; although the use of a supporting tool is essential, it should support and not replace the judgment and business intuition of PPMT members. The confidence of the PPMT in its own decisions is critical to securing the organisation's buy-in and support. The PPMT needs to strike the right balance given the business culture, and adjust the PPM process accordingly.

PPMT members should consider the various scenarios and be prepared to discuss and demonstrate the consequences of the options presented. Maintaining a true cross-functional perspective on the part of the PPMT becomes particularly important during this analysis period of the PPM process. Should the PPMT lose the balance provided by its participating membership, analysis of resource issues will become superficial and ineffective.

10.2 Authorising projects and resources

At this stage decisions are made, validated and communicated as to the utilisation of available resources. This focuses available resources on the priority work of the organisation and eliminates the overallocation of resources.

The steps in this stage include:

1 determining and authorising the planned utilisation of resources
2 making the hard decisions
3 validating with the portfolio sponsor and notifying project sponsors
4 communicating decisions to the project 'community'
5 managing and sustaining the project portfolio process

10.2.1   Determining and authorising the planned utilisation of resources

The PPMT recommends which projects should continue, which should be postponed for future implementation, and which should be cancelled or should not proceed beyond the planning phase. This focuses the work of the organisation on the priority projects based on its business strategies.

This is the most significant moment within the PPM process. All the process activities have been conducted to position the PPMT to make the most valuable optimisation decisions: creating an environment of clear roles and parameters; establishing a prioritisation process that consciously aligns project work with business strategies; reconciling resource availability and resource demand based on the prioritisation of projects; and focusing and planning resources on the projects that most effectively advance the business strategies of the organisation.

The view of the PPMT ranges beyond the individual resource authorisation perspective to a broader project portfolio perspective. The PPMT brings together the optimisation tactics identified by the individual team members and the 'what if' scenarios created to view the impact of various optimisation tactics. The PPMT applies its business intuition to the fact based information that has been developed throughout the process.

10.2.2   Making the hard decisions

The toughest decision is drawing the cutoff line, as in the example shown in Figure 40.

Projects falling above the line are 'eligible' for resource assignments and those falling below the line are likely either to be placed on hold for future consideration or cancelled. Although the PPMT makes the 'go/kill/hold/fix' decisions, not all optimisation tactics are that simple or straightforward. There are a lot of in-between decisions.

Project name	Priority #	Gross resources (FTE)	Timescale
ABC	1	24	
XYZ	2	5	
Star	3	130	
T-shot	4	67	
Waldo	5	12	
Warrior	6	15	
ATF	7	30	
Eclipse	8	56	
Raker	9	10	

Cutoff

Figure 40 Making the hard decisions: drawing lines of eligibility (example)

The PPMT must be ready to manage various complexities in its decision making and in many ways it is an issue of balance. For example, the PPMT can make project schedule or scope adjustments to optimise the organisation's resource capacity, by postponing project start dates or waiting until existing staff available or new staff can be hired. Other adjustments include:

- starting projects earlier; putting resources to work that are currently available
- starting some phases now, shifting other phases of the effort out to later
- rebalancing the organisation's resource schedules
- authorising some scope activities without giving a global authorisation; for example, deploying systems locally, but holding off on worldwide deployment

Resource information alone is not enough for the complex decisions that the PPMT must make. The PPMT must also consider a life cycle timetable which helps to position phases for optimal use of phase-specific resources, such as those provided by lab technicians or market analysts. The priority ranking of projects allows the PPMT to focus on optimisation of the highest-priority project work.

Project managers and project sponsors both need to balance project assignments, ensuring that the same project manager does not become overloaded with a group of high-priority projects. The project type or domain allows the PPMT to balance the portfolio to ensure that one type of project does not usurp availability of resources for other types; for example, ensuring that infrastructure projects are not constantly 'bumped' in order to accomplish R&D projects. Further consideration must also be given to interdependencies between projects, ensuring that the PPMT clearly understands the consequences of its decisions for other projects in the portfolio. The PPMT must also consider specific output dependencies between projects, specifically when:

- a project is dependent on the output of another project within the same project portfolio
- a project is dependent on the output of another project from a different project portfolio within the company
- a project is contributing a specific output to another project, whether in the same portfolio or in a separate portfolio within the company

The project interdependencies for the above are not resource dependencies, but rather output or deliverable based dependencies. Assessment of the consequences of optimisation tactics should include the effect on the schedules of other projects that are dependent on the output of the optimised project. A change in the date by which a specific interface is required in a project should be explicitly communicated during the optimisation process to ensure open acknowledgement of schedule conflicts.

The portfolio sponsor becomes involved when an optimisation tactic recommended by the PPMT affects projects in other portfolios. Typically the portfolio sponsor acts as liaison with the sponsor of the affected portfolio, escalates issues to executive management that cannot be resolved at the portfolio level, and supports the PPMT in implementing the solution.

The whole portfolio management process needs to be a team effort. The challenges anticipated in optimisation account for the membership characteristics of the PPMT. These include:

- project advocates – bringing a project perspective to optimisation
- functional advocates – understanding the resource management impact of optimisation decisions
- all members having senior management and executive experience – helping maintain the focus on alignment with business strategies
- PMO manager – providing information support
- PPMT leader – focusing the team's efforts for maximum efficiency
- portfolio sponsor – guiding the PPMT with a more global perspective

The ultimate responsibility for portfolio optimisation decisions lies with the PPMT leader. Optimisation is best executed and supported by the organisation when reflected as a team based decision. The PMO assumes an important role in providing timely and accurate information to the PPMT. The various members of the PPMT provide the appropriate perspective and advocacy for their project or functional area. Any divisiveness and unwillingness to accept shared responsibility for the decisions made only serve to undermine the PPM process.

Once projects have been authorised to proceed, resources are assigned based on the organisation's decision making framework and culture. The bottom line is that the PPMT has a central role in either the making of or support of resource assignments. The initial resource commitments should be secured based on the detailed plans and project priorities as reflected in the project registry.

The PPMT does not want to take optimisation decisions to the portfolio sponsor for approval, only to find out later that the resource commitments could not support the decisions made. Project managers normally attempt to resolve any resource issues or inconsistencies with their project teams and project sponsors. Resource issues that cannot be resolved within the project team should be escalated to the PPMT through the project sponsor. Resource conflicts should be resolved, where possible, prior to submitting detailed information to the project registry.

The PPMT leader will regularly validate utilisation recommendations with the portfolio sponsor. In order to facilitate the cycle of validation, information should be available in the project registry for simple and direct review. The PMO should maintain a 'what if' version of the registry, which is used to evaluate various optimisation tactics, view the consequences for the overall portfolio, and capture recommended decisions for validation. The 'what if' version of the project registry should not be made public to the entire organisation – it should be available to PPMT members for evaluation purposes.

Optimisation decisions are made by the PPMT. Once again, these should be quorum decisions, and not delegated to anyone else. The PMO ensures that recommendation decisions are entered into the project registry. The PPMT leader prepares for validation with the portfolio sponsor.

This optimisation process can be more difficult for a new PPMT at the beginning. As this process is implemented in the organisation, it will be discovered that project work is under way that needs to be cancelled or placed on hold. The PPMT must take responsibility for these difficult decisions and work within the political confines of the organisation to reshape the look of project work.

At times the PPMT leader may feel reluctant to push to the hard decision of 'drawing the line' that indicates which projects will be authorised for resource assignment. The portfolio sponsor should support the PPMT in this role, not take the role away from the PPMT leader. The 'what if' version of the project registry held by the PMO should be the focus. This facilitates the decision making process and ensures that it remains fact based – always considering the impact of proposed decisions on the rest of the project portfolio.

The optimisation exercise is a regular item on the PPMT agenda and is accomplished every time new project work is considered. Carrying it out in small increments takes away the potential for it to become an overwhelming part of the PPMT's job.

10.2.3 Validating with the portfolio sponsor and notifying project sponsors

The PPMT reviews the decisions made with the portfolio sponsor for approval or reconsideration. This ensures commitment from the leadership of the organisation to both the priorities and the implementation of prioritised project work.

The key aspect of validation is to demonstrate the impact of the optimisation decisions of the PPMT. This can be shown using a resource management tool or a PPM software tool. The PPMT must be prepared to exhibit or show the benefits and tradeoffs of the optimisation 'what if' scenarios. It is not necessary for the PPMT to revisit every decision made leading to the optimised project portfolio.

The portfolio sponsor must validate or approve the optimisation so as to understand the support the PPMT needs to implement its decisions. The portfolio sponsor looks for any inconsistencies between the recommended resource utilisation and the business strategies of the organisation, and reviews those projects that will not be accomplished. In many organisations the portfolio sponsor also identifies and reviews specific resource implications such as temporary contract requirements, long term hiring requirements and cross-training opportunities among others.

Over time the PPMT will become more experienced and acquire expertise in optimisation decision making, so that only significant issues need to be addressed with the portfolio sponsor. In circumstances where significant or repetitious adjustments are made to the PPMT's decisions, it is suggested that there is a need to re-examine the portfolio environment. Such adjustments can be as a result of:

- project domains not being correctly structured
- business strategies needing review for inadvertent exclusion of important considerations

- prioritisation criteria needing adjustment to more closely represent the business strategies
- the scoring model needing revision to more accurately reflect the decision points for project consideration
- functional or project managers not entering appropriate, accurate, or adequate information into the project registry
- the PMO staff might needing training in project management support technology or skills

The portfolio sponsor must be given the basis of the PPMT's decisions, so as to be able to provide the needed support. It is important for the sponsor to 'stay above the fray' of the optimisation challenges and confirm the conscious alignment of the optimised portfolio with the business strategies of the organisation. The approved projects appear as such in the project registry.

The portfolio sponsor must work closely with the PPMT during the early stages of implementation to ensure that the entire team understands the process and arrives at a common practice. The PPMT must not be shy about raising questions or concerns about the validation process and outcomes during the first few cycles of validation. This allows for open communication and a clear understanding of the portfolio sponsor's expectations.

The success of this validation, and the subsequent implementation of the optimised solutions, are dependent on a unified approach by the PPMT and the portfolio sponsor to the overall project 'community'.

Validation and issue resolution with the portfolio sponsor must be a regularly scheduled event. The PPMT leader must strive to keep the amount of optimisation to be considered in a single validation session to a reasonable level. This is most effectively accomplished by ensuring that optimisation and validation happen as regularly and as frequently as is practical. The validation process is most effective when the PPMT leader understand the portfolio sponsor's preferred method of communication and consistently presents data accordingly

10.2.4   Communicating decisions to the project 'community'

The authorised decisions on resource utilisation are made available to the project 'community'. This ensures that persons available to provide project resources understand and schedule their work according to authorised project schedules.

PPM best practice demands that the PPMT follow a predefined communication process. The framework should address exactly how resource authorisation and assignment will be communicated. The PPMT must ensure the decisions are communicated to project and functional managers, in the context of each individually affected project.

It is courteous to first inform project teams of the resource utilisation decisions, before the entire project 'community' is notified. The PPMT must communicate the exact nature of the resource authorisation directly to project managers and their teams, making clear whether the resource requirements have been authorised exactly as requested, or whether only limited resources have been authorised as part of the optimisation decision, or whether a project has been placed on hold or cancelled. All project managers must be informed of the status of their projects and of the reasoning behind the decisions.

Communication of resource authorisation decisions must be taken seriously as an important role for the PMO. Continued communication, including the encouragement of feedback, is a powerful way to promote the improvement, propagation and organisational acceptance of the PPM process.

10.2.5 Managing and sustaining the project portfolio process

Once the PPM process has been established, it is essential to maintain current and accurate data to support the ongoing decision process. This maintenance activity must create and communicate a realistic picture of portfolio projects and resource requirements so that the PPMT can effectively manage the portfolio.

Key decisions resulting from this process are whether to:

- solicit and/or add new projects
- 'go/kill/hold/fix' projects
- make schedule, scope, or resource adjustments to existing projects
- reprioritise existing projects
- adjust the portfolio balance/mix

The primary activities that must be engaged in to sustain the PPM process are:

- tracking portfolio events
- balancing the portfolio

Portfolio events are tracked via status collection, which provides feedback so as to communicate project progress against the registered plan. Typically, status is summarised as Green, Amber or Red depending on schedule or cost variance, resource utilisation actuals and forecasts versus planned, and outstanding issues.

Functional and project managers must continuously fine-tune and adjust milestone and deliverable dates and resource estimates as they obtain increasingly accurate information regarding the project and the resources required to accomplish it.

As indicated earlier, the portfolio management process often begins for an individual project when very little is known about it. At this point in time, portfolio analysis and decisions are based on estimates and target dates. As the project progresses, enough information is eventually generated to make firm schedule and resource commitments. Even so, as deliverables are produced and actuals tracked, forecasts begin to change based on this new information.

The net result is a dynamic portfolio that is constantly changing. The PMO manager and the PPMT must continuously evaluate portfolio performance and act accordingly to maintain the optimal balance of projects and efficiently utilise the organisation's resources to accomplish this. Portfolio metrics must be captured and documented to guide the PPMT decision making process.

Over the course of time, many factors impact the portfolio and the projects that initially comprise it.

Market conditions and opportunities change, as well as economic conditions and forecasts. Therefore, the business environment must be constantly evaluated to ensure the organisation is still working on the right projects and/or the right mix of projects. As a result, domain and project prioritisation adjustments are often required or desired. These adjustments may be in the form of how domains are defined, funding or headcount allocated to each domain, domain admittance criteria, or weights given to certain types of projects.

Throughout the life of the portfolio, projects are completed and perhaps some are cancelled. These projects must be closed out and removed from the portfolio. This, in turn, creates opportunities for new projects, which must be prioritised and if appropriate added to the portfolio. A portfolio review must conducted periodically to ensure that the proper number and proportion of projects are included in the portfolio.

Evaluating the business environment and conducting portfolio reviews may also result in reprioritising projects and adjusting the schedule, scope or resources relating to individual projects.

PART IV

Embed the Project Portfolio Management capability

The greatest challenge in PPM deployment is embedding and sustaining the capability so that the necessary PPM benefits are achieved by the organisation. In this part of the book we suggest ways for companies to achieve oversight and sustain their PPM capability as a part of cultural performance. We discuss and analyse culture, and how a PPM solution should be managed with a cultural buy-in through a successful change management process. Further, the development of a knowledge management strategy is discussed which, together with benefits management, can enable a cultural acceptance of the PPM process.

CHAPTER 11

Embed the PPM culture and capabilities

The word 'culture' is used a great deal by management and organisational development practitioners to describe the climate and practices that organisations develop around their handling of people. A great deal of work has been done on corporate culture and its relationship to business performance.

For our purposes, culture in a corporate context can be defined as a system of values, norms, and ideas, shared by a group of people, that when taken together provide a design for thinking, living and potential action. By 'values' is meant the shared assumptions of what ought to be or, in other words, what a group believes to be right and desirable. 'Norms' relate to rules and guidelines that set out expected behavior in various circumstances. So corporate culture reflects the values of the founders, underpins the vision or mission of the firm, establishes the main operating orientation of the company, and provides the basis for a shared identity for company members. Its importance lies in the fact that not only does culture constitute a kind of interpersonal glue that holds an organisation together, but it can also function as an informal control mechanism that may help coordinate employee efforts.

11.1 The importance of organisational culture

There are many different ways of thinking about organisational culture and ways of changing it, which you should be able to find in any one of a number of good textbooks on the subject. Here, we confine ourselves to emphasising that real change in how things are done inside an organisation, as required by the move to a PPM approach, cannot happen unless its culture is changed first. But corporate culture is a difficult thing to pin down and even harder to change because it reflects the implicit values, norms and behaviours of an organisation.

Anticipating and accommodating change proactively, rather than reactively, is the most effective course of action. Project managers responsible for planning and implementing these systems should make sure to build an effective change management process into the project plan from the beginning. PPM capability can be embedded as part of the culture of the organisation only if managed through a sound change management plan.

11.2 Embedding PPM capability through a sound change management plan

The introduction of the PPM process and system is usually disruptive to the status quo in companies or workgroups. This is especially important to consider when planning PPM implementation because by the very nature of the process it can change long-established business processes and practices.

As described earlier, anticipating, accommodating and accepting PPM as a change programme, proactively rather than reactively, is the most effective way of embedding cultural acceptance. Project managers responsible for planning and implementing this process and system should make sure that they build effective change management into the project plan from the beginning.

The simplest definition of change management is 'making change in a planned and managed fashion'. Today's proliferation of digital media and changes in technology are making the conscious practice of change management more important than it was only five or ten years ago.

Even more fundamentally, it is important to understand that change management is a *political* process that requires corporate managers and project managers to share their vision of how users' lives will change (presumably for the better) because of a new system, and then get the users to agree to implement the changes necessary to make it work.

For PPM deployment to be successful and embedded within the organisation, change management planning should begin as early as possible, and should itself be treated as a project. Gaining buy-in from users is vital, however, because people become comfortable with the status quo, and often find ways to resist or sabotage change, particularly if they feel uninvolved.

When confronted by the possibility of a new system, the first thing most people want to know is, 'What's in it for me?'. It is by soliciting their concerns up front, addressing them in your plans, and then implementing incremental changes whenever the schedule permits, that you will be most effective. Although such a deliberate approach may take more time, in the end it will help you win internal advocates, instead of enemies.

In a round-table discussion we held on the subject of PPM, a financial institution IT manager said, 'Applying change management practice within the IT division was one of the key success factor for the deployment of the PPM system.' He further explained that, 'Even the best technology can fail, while a mediocre low-tech solution can succeed if we can get the buy-in from the stakeholders.'

The real art of change management is predetermining the effects of the PPM process and technology on the people who must work with it, anticipating their objections, then being prepared to overcome those objections when they arise. This is easiest to achieve if change starts from the ground up and is supported from the top down, because users feel involved. Of course this is not always the case; often the demand for PPM systems is driven by management's quest for business performance. Under these circumstances, there are several ways change can occur. Either those affected can be persuaded that change is (a) in their best interests, and (b) inevitable, or in the absence of that, (c) as the project manager, you may need to impose some form of 'monitoring and reinforcing change'.

Throughout the book we have reiterated that we cannot succeed without the backing of senior leadership. Our work with companies highlights the fact that the single most critical factor for success is the support of senior management. When senior management is supportive, breakdowns do not get viewed as putting a stop to the project. It is more effective to treat a breakdown from the perspective that something must be *missing*, rather than that something must be *wrong*. When you approach something from the perspective of 'right' and 'wrong', you start to look for who is responsible for what's 'wrong', so that blame and finger pointing can become the background against which you are trying to accomplish your goal. This tends to erode the relationship between management and users, on the one hand, and those who are accountable for bringing about this new way of doing business, on the other, and to rob the initiative of its power.

Another obvious but subtle problem that can appear is that executives don't speak the same language as PPM system users. In this new world of PPM, we are not only looking for projects that are managed well, but also for projects that are right for the firm. So a partnership has been formed between the project oriented people in the PMO and the business oriented approach represented by executives. Our experience has been that the design and implementation of a PPM capability have often been derailed by the simple situation that the two groups do not speak the same language (as well as having a different focus).

For instance, in the PMO, when you report to others about how your project is going, do you focus on schedule and costs? Do you talk about resource utilisation or scope changes? Surely these are important items. As project managers we are taught to communicate these key items to management as a measure of whether the project is progressing successfully. They are still important as a gauge of project health. But they don't always reflect the full story with regard to impact on the business.

When communicating to executives, you need to focus on the terms that reflect how the project is contributing to the larger set of objectives of the enterprise. How is the project contributing to growth, competitive advantage, revenue and cash flow, effective utilisation of all resources, and key strategic initiatives? Focus more on benefits, revenue, and ROI than on costs. The project end date may not be as important as the window of opportunity.

For each person that you communicate with, think about how that person gets measured and views success. Then design custom communications for each, in the language that they use. One of the first tasks of the PPMT will be to develop a set of terms and metrics which will form the basis of the communication stream that supports the PPM process.

Our own observation and feedback from clients have shown that incremental change is less risky and more favourably looked upon than the 'big bang' approach, and that success in the deployment of the project can add tremendous credibility.

11.3 Sustaining PPM capability through a knowledge management (KM) strategy

As PPM represents a new way of doing business we need to create a PPM knowledge management (KM) strategy as part of change management. We define knowledge management as the offering of a comprehensive series of accelerated learning interventions that will increase organisational knowledge of the PPM initiative. This would involve the conversion of knowledge into applicable skills. Examples of learning interventions which can accelerate staff learning are depicted in Figure 41. There is no one direct way of transferring knowledge and skills, but a combination of ways that need to be selected to fit the culture of the organisation and its learning style.

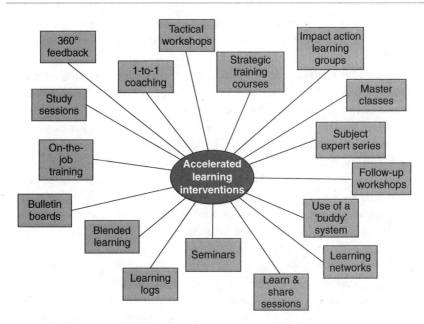

Figure 41 Accelerated learning interventions (examples)

The PPM initiative, with its organisational impact, requires the company to implement new roles, processes and automation. The change can appear daunting for many employees whose first experience with the new technique is in a training class.

Dissemination of knowledge must be planned with the recognition that it is a critical mechanism for getting employees to adopt change. The extent of change that can come with PPM means that dissemination of knowledge must start with the development of a knowledge management strategy. Many organisations do not do so. In some companies we have at least seen a training strategy developed, which is far better than no strategy at all.

A thoughtful KM strategy defines the desired end results and identifies risks and issues – including change management issues. Creating a KM strategy helps create a knowledge implementation plan that addresses change and delivers the desired end results through accelerated learning interventions.

Finally, a KM strategy is a communication tool and a motivator for managers and trainees – both groups will appreciate the foresight and insight it provides. A KM strategy that addresses the changes facing an organisation helps ensure the changes are adopted when learning has been completed.

There are some significant change management techniques that need to be included in the KM strategy. An important consideration is that of educating people about why the change is occurring. It is well understood that employees are more motivated to support an initiative when they understand the goals of the initiative. The goals of the PPM initiative should be defined well in advance of the learning event, when the business case for the initiative is developed. The business case is the basis for describing why the changes associated with the PPM initiative are occurring.

In addition to making known the high-level goals of the initiative, goals should also be defined by role, so that each person knows how his or her function supports the project. Every person should be educated on the goals of every role – with the 'whole picture', employees will understand their role better, and will collaborate more effectively with their peers after the learning event.

As PPM is a process based deployment, the learning event needs to be comprehensive and to present a well defined PPM process, so that all roles are clearly identified and all responsibilities are specified. PPM requires the right mix of people, process and system – without all three, the impact will be less than optimal. With the thorough definition of the PPM process, or at least the portion being implemented, all the roles that are required to support the process are easily identifiable. With the process and roles identified, responsibilities by role can then be defined. This becomes the source material for building lesson plans.

Training by role keeps the learning grounded and focused. Role based learning forces trainers and facilitators to 'keep it real' by focusing on the actions taken day to day by specific people. It also minimises the learning time for each role group. This ensures there are no 'holes' in the process when it is rolled out.

Not to be overlooked is learning for executive managers. Executive participation must start early in a PPM implementation, with the definition of goals and the outputs needed for achieving the goals. Imagine the disappointment of getting all the employees of an organisation working together on a new process, only to have it deliver no results because executives are not trained on how to hold up their end.

Learning is always an opportunity to reinvigorate the workforce. Unfortunately, change often induces fear, and employees often also experience uncertainty and doubt about the implementation of PPM. In particular, employees fear the visibility, accountability and oversight that come with a portfolio approach to managing projects and resources.

If the company adopts a 'pure' training approach, asking trainees to passively receive a new set of policies and procedures to follow, this can exacerbate the negative perceptions mentioned above. Training that simply gets the employees into line fails to address the angst of change, limiting the effectiveness of the training. Worse, it fails to capitalise on an opportunity for the organisation to learn and continuously improve.

To reinforce the point once again, the organisation should strive to develop a knowledge management strategy that supports learning interventions and makes each training event a two-way learning opportunity. These events should be an opportunity to receive input from employees for the fine-tuning of the processes as the employees learn new functions. In concert with transferring knowledge, learning should also encourage participation, feedback and further innovation.

11.4 Project benefits management (PBM) as an enabler for embedding PPM capability

Benefits management is the activity of identifying, optimising and tracking the expected benefit from business change to ensure that they are achieved. It is a core activity running throughout a change or transformational programme and beyond its immediate conclusion.

Benefits management therefore covers:

- defining the business benefits expected from PPM, ensuring that the nature of these benefits is clearly understood and accepted by all those responsible for them and involved in delivering them
- understanding the offset of benefits against the cost and risks involved in achieving them
- planning how benefits will be achieved and measured
- allocating responsibility for successful delivery of benefits
- monitoring the achievement of benefits as systematically as the tracking of costs
- assessing how successfully the benefits have been delivered

Benefits management is thus an end-to-end process from initial identification of PPM benefits, through delivery and monitoring, to subsequent assessment of what has been achieved.

11.4.1 Realising the benefits

The real power of benefits realisation is when it is linked to a PPM process.

Increased project activity is good news and should result in a corresponding rise in value being delivered back to the organisation.

Yet results indicate that while companies are delivering some value back to the organisation, benefits are also being leaked away. Most businesses have more opportunities than they have available financial and human resources to engage with.

It is critical that limited resources be committed only to initiatives likely to produce the most advantage for the business. It is essential that organisations adopt a strategy that enables them to identify and put a value on each proposal under consideration.

A benefits driven measure of project success means greater account-ability and raised expectations at every stage of the project life cycle. It requires increased project governance, from scrutiny of the business case, to essential monitoring and measuring during the project and after completion.

Without this rigorous approach to benefits tracking, organisations seri-ously risk unaccountable benefits leakage and will continue failing to deliver on projects.

Here are six key principles for achieving economic value:

1 Adopt an integrated governance framework, driven by the board, which starts from the business case and ends with measuring the actual value.
2 Align all initiatives clearly with the business strategy.
3 Establish an organisation-wide prioritisation process that objectively and continuously evaluates projects to maximise the value of the investment.
4 Clearly define individual accountability for realising benefits, including integrating benefits with organisational plans and budgets.
5 Control benefits leakage by clearly defining the anticipated value, how it will be realised and when – monitor and reassess regularly throughout the project.
6 Recognise the links between strategy and project execution, and develop appropriate capability, capacity and risk models.

11.4.2 Project benefits management roles

Three key PBM roles can be defined:

- *Project sponsors* ensure adherence to the PBM process. They validate the business case and approve the project plan. They monitor the progress of the project against the plan and ensure that the project's initial business case is revalidated at appropriate intervals during project execution. They close the project and hand over responsibility for benefits delivery to respective project beneficiaries.

- *Project managers* are authorised by sponsors to plan and execute projects. They ensure that project plans are optimised and executed in accordance with PBM principles. This may mean, for example, that the timing and sequencing of specific project activities is altered to maximise early return of benefits. They produce project progress reports on work, schedule, cost, scope and benefits potential, to be reviewed against the business case.
- *Project beneficiaries* ensure that business benefits resulting from the project are defined in accordance with PBM principles. This means that project benefits are broken down into appropriate basic parameters, with clear metrics, valuation, ownership and timing. They ensure validity of benefits statements throughout the life of the project. They accept personal accountability for the accuracy of benefits statements and ultimately for the realisation of project benefits.

The three roles are interdependent and extend throughout the project life cycle.

11.4.3   Project benefits management processes and tools

Project benefits management (PBM) describes the roles, responsibilities, processes and tools that optimise ongoing investments in projects. PBM is a part of economic value management. The deployment of a PPM process and systems needs to be seen as an exercise in economic value management. When it is considered in this light it gets the full support of stakeholders.

Projects are investments. Like all investments there are anticipated costs, benefits and risks. These are defined in the project's *business case*. The business case justifies the funding of the project. The *sponsor* ensures that the business case is based on a realistic comparison of the estimated project costs with the anticipated benefits, expressed in financial terms.

Sponsors oversee the development of both the cost and the benefit component of this comparison. The sponsor's fundamental role is to ensure validation and alignment between the project and the benefits throughout the project life cycle.

The work breakdown structure (WBS) is an important tool used by the project team, under the direction of the project sponsor, for identifying the project scope and breaking it down to a level of detail where credible cost and schedule estimates can be developed. At this level of detail project deliverable accountability can be assigned to the project manager and the project team members.

The key tool and technique used by the sponsor and project beneficiaries to analyse anticipated project benefits is the *benefits breakdown structure* (BBS). This structure reflects the total business benefit broken down into its constituent parts. These are called *basic benefit parameters.* The BBS technique allows project impact on business performance to be traced to specific beneficiaries, the impact measured and its value to the business established. This serves to identify and firmly commit project beneficiaries to the project.

Benefits realisation profiles illustrate the delivery of project benefits over time. The benefits profile associated with individual projects is key for sponsors in terms of project planning, prioritisation and allocation of critical resources across the entire portfolio. For instance, the performance of projects assumed to have long term recurring benefits will be measured in terms of time to reach breakeven. Cost-to-complete matters for some projects, whereas time-to-complete is an issue for other projects with finite benefits, within a limited window of opportunity.

11.4.4 Benefits realisation and PPM deployment

A benefits approach is based on one simple assertion:

> Your real goal when making any business investment is to achieve benefits. So long as you can achieve these within accepted constraints, you can be flexible on the specifics of the solution.

Those with business responsibilities don't argue with this assertion, but the implications are not reflected in the majority of projects we see.

Asking a few simple questions can check how serious your organisation is about realising benefits:

- Does everyone have the same understanding of what a benefit is?
- Have required benefits been expressed in measurable terms in early project documentation such as project mandates, requirement specifications, business cases?
- Do project reports show measurable progress in delivering benefits?

In environments where the answer to all these questions is 'No', we generally find that benefits are not a primary goal, but something that people expect to emerge from activities and products that form the main project drivers. Responsibility for benefits realisation is often undefined and is only addressed after project delivery.

Where you can answer 'Yes' to all the above questions, you have a benefits driven project environment, with business considerations driving technology implementation.

Effective communication is at the heart of benefits realisation. Stakeholders need help with the unambiguous expression of their benefit needs in ways that project staff can understand. This aids clear discussion around feasibility. The objective is 'no surprises'.

We define a benefit as 'some improvement in performance of value to a stakeholder', since:

- Without an improvement, you have no benefit.
- Without a stakeholder, you have no benefit.

If an improvement can be perceived, then it can be quantified. At first people generally find it difficult to quantify because they have not learnt how to envision outcomes in performance improvement terms. Our techniques centre on the definition of performance dimensions which are simply means to communicate effectively using numbers.

Planning for early delivery of benefits is essential for keeping projects in touch with reality. Most stakeholders place greater value on a small improvement next week, than on a modest percentage probability of the 'complete solution' in two years' time. Structuring project work packages for evolutionary delivery of benefits is different to planning for incremental delivery of products. However, it allows funding for work packages to be linked directly to benefits delivery and reduces levels of financial risk.

When reporting, simple graphical techniques are available for presenting comprehensive performance data in concise formats, that is, with more pictures and fewer words in reports. The management issues centre on what improvement has been delivered and what improvement is planned, by when.

Contracts and payment regimes can also be constructed for payment based on performance delivered. Why should you want to pay for anything that does not add demonstrable value?

Finally, needs change as a result of feedback from implementation and from external sources. Continual re-evaluation of benefits is necessary to check whether they continue to be valued by stakeholders.

Adopting this approach to benefits realisation has the following potential benefits to stakeholders:

- The business has greater visibility and control over the business impact of projects.
- Benefits expectations are made more explicit, with less reliance on hope.
- The squandering of resources is lessened.
- Project staff have a clearer idea of what success looks like.
- Tying work packages to benefits delivery minimises the level of financial risk. If benefits cannot be delivered for part of a project budget, why risk the whole budget?
- There is less reliance on reviewing project documentation to ensure projects are on track; the results show effectiveness or otherwise.
- Innovation is stimulated. New ideas should not be technically constrained to the chosen solution but be evaluated for impact on the desired benefits.
- Business cases based on benefits are easier to construct and get approval for than those focused on technical solutions.
- Teams work to provide an integrated, benefits focused effect, across training, processes and technology.

11.5   PPM process sustainability and support

It is important to provide process oversight and support to ensure staff are properly educated to contribute to the portfolio management process. Project and resource templates help provide structure and consistency in the data collection and reporting process. Audits of projects and processes ensure staff are undertaking the right activities in the right way. These activities all contribute to the establishment of a consistent, repeatable process, which is instrumental to effective long term portfolio management. Process oversight and support are provided by the PMO and enforced by the PPMT and functional managers.

Adequate and appropriate training is required throughout the organisation to support ongoing management of the PPM process. The initial training will not sustain the PPMT and many factors will indicate the need for more and different training, such as:

- the evolving role of the PPMT
- refinement of PPM processes
- reduced dependency on outside resources
- adaptation of the process to organisational dynamics

- availability of new and enhanced software or software features
- practical experience of project and programme training processes
- new development life cycles
- significant change in the business strategies or business culture

Training should be practical in nature – do not train on concepts only, and develop a training schedule that allows all new members of the organisation to be assimilated into the standard processes. Members of the organisation who are well versed in the process should be regularly included in the training of new members, to allow the seasoned employee to be exposed to fresh ideas and new employees to be given experience based application tips.

Online training should be accompanied by demonstrations of practical skills application. All training opportunities in the project, programme and portfolio management skills areas should be well coordinated and explicitly call out the interrelationship of the supporting processes. The training must include a well developed 'mentor' approach.

PPMT members bear the responsibility for carefully watching for required training when there is evidence of weakness in any supporting or related process in the organisation that might hinder the implementation of the PPM process.

Project sponsors, portfolio sponsors, the PPMT leader and PPMT members should constantly watch for PPM process performance weakness and aggressively train to correct it. Even though PPMT members do not bear direct responsibility for outlying processes (budgeting, hiring, evaluation, and so on) they must proactively work with those responsible for project delivery to ensure that weakness in the performance of these outlying processes does not hinder or stifle the ongoing improvement of the PPM process.

CHAPTER 12

PPM business scenarios

In this chapter we map out some of the typical business scenarios that we have encountered when implementing PPM. We discuss from a high-level viewpoint the typical business challenges faced, the solution and processes implemented, and then round off with how the business has benefited.

12.1 Scenario 1: establishing a repeatable and scalable PPM process

12.1.1 The business challenges

Your primary objective is to build and establish a repeatable and scalable PPM process, to increase market share.

What problems do you face? The enterprise has inherited multiple project planning and resourcing infrastructures across a number of sites. Processes are linked in the short term via a series of fragmented spread-sheets and in-house legacy applications all covering core aspects of the business including business plans, operational deployment, and fore-casting as well as project resource demand and supply. These inconsistent systems and infrastructures impact every level of the organisation.

Typical problems you face are:

- *Lack of business synergy*: Management does not have access to accurate real-time information to help identify key problem areas. For example, the lack of visibility of milestones impacts on the business's ability to forecast and budget.
- *Poor understanding of resourcing capability*: Because of multiple internal systems and processes, resource managers depend on quarterly staffing plans to understand the types of resources required to meet future needs. This problem is compounded further by an unreliable and inefficient method of securing people via verbal networking and bartering. These informal processes limit the ability to optimise staffing

levels, which inevitability leads to lower utilisation rates, skills short-ages and lower profitability.

- *Inconsistent planning*: A fragmented planning methodology and an inability to systematically examine and fine-tune multiple project scenarios and assumptions lead to regular unforeseen roadblocks. Lack of project transparency means that project and executive managers are unable to forecast and accurately plan new projects and assign people (resources) with the right skills. Moreover, poor planning prevents management from effectively driving new products to market.
- *Disparate technical infrastructure*: Multiple systems have created a technical jungle. A single standard does not exist and this lack of technical synergy prevents the organisation from working by a consistent method. This impacts on executive ability to source real-time information, forcing decisions to be based on estimations or, at worst, guesswork.

12.1.2 The business solution

Underpinning the drive to establish a repeatable and scalable PPM process is alignment of strategic and operational visibility through better planning and management of resources, in order to ensure ongoing competitive advantage for the company.

The PPM process is to be implemented as part of a phased approach. The first stage is to identify which are the 'real' projects, who is working on what, and to determine where productivity deficits are occurring. The second stage is to take this information and rewire the planning and resource management system by implementing a fully functional PPM process. A critical part of the implementation is to ensure that the process configuration is wrapped around the organisation's business strategy. The goal is to ensure that for the first time, executives have a real-time view of the true status of the key factors that determine the health of the business, from top-line strategy down through to departments, portfolios, programmes, plans, milestones, business objectives and KPIs.

12.1.3 The business benefits

A repeatable and scalable PPM process is designed to deliver a better understanding of the business – fusing together the strategic and operational processes by maximising efficiency and seeing benefits such as:

- *Increased enterprise visibility*: Increased visibility of primary business functions enables executives to make top-level decisions that are based on coherent factual information, presented and accessed simply and delivered in real time. This visibility gives executives a top-down insight into each department, their projects, their costs and who is responsible for each. As a result, executives are able to make strategic and operational decisions quickly, which can be adjusted as changes to projects in the pipeline arise.
- *Improved organisational productivity*: The PPM process delivers immediate efficiency and effectiveness through improved project planning, resourcing and real-time management information. The goal is to ensure that the right people, with the right skills, at the right location, at the right costs, are doing the right work. For example, efficiency gains include:
  - *uniform planning and resourcing processes*: enhancing the planning process through the integration and optimisation of skills and resource schedules with faster, more integrated project planning
  - *process and application standardisation*: providing a single point of entry that keeps information consistent, current and complete and also ensures that staff work within only one framework
  - *real-time management information reporting*: implementation of a powerful management information framework ensuring: (1) no more manual assembling of data – information is sourced from one central database, which massively reduces reporting time-scales; (2) where once executives had to wait days or even weeks, they are now able to produce performance reports, financial forecasts and resourcing needs analysis in real time. The management information framework ensures that the business is able to react quicker and more effectively to meet changing market dynamics.
- *Real-time role based views*: Project portfolio information is now tailored to support many different business areas and disciplines, sourced from one single powerful real-time data repository. For example:
  - *Executives*: They can now roll up into one single environment an end-to-end view of the entire set of the business's projects. 'What if' scenario capability gives executives the ability see the effects of key changes as part of the whole strategic corporate perspective. Potential roadblocks and resource shortages can be anticipated and organised for before they occur.
  - *Portfolio and programme managers*: They can now reap the benefits of improved project data which helps them manage their portfolios in a proactive and more effective manner. They are

now able to gain a quick insight into the impact of delaying or accelerating a project's schedule, and use software generated reports to view information from various perspectives so that they can make business-critical decisions. The PPM process has given them real-time analysis of which projects are slipping or misaligned, and whether identified budgets cover the work, as well as enabling them to plan multiple portfolio scenarios requirements for time, costs and skills.

o *Resource managers*: The PPM process enables them to start looking ahead at their staff workloads, not only by project or month, but also by discipline, skills and expertise. The process has delivered a single real-time view of the resource allocation and planning processes, enabling them to create realistic schedules and make better, more informed decisions about altering these schedules when project priorities or scopes change.

o *Project managers*: They now have access to a comprehensive set of reports that enable them to communicate important project information to key project stakeholders, customers, project team members and the business.

12.2 Scenario 2: creating an IT profit centre by strategically aligning the IT project delivery process with the business

12.2.1 The business challenges

Your primary objective is to use the PPM process to successfully align all IT project investments with the overall corporate strategy to deliver maximum business value. It is essential to create a service based IT profit centre and deliver more strategic, business driven solutions in order to facilitate revenue growth, and adhere to new governance and regulatory initiatives, all while providing superior IT support and maintaining critical applications. It is essential for IT to resolve the disconnect with executive peers and provide stakeholders with real-time visibility of progress and of the problems that hamper the delivery of expected results.

What problems do you face? The IT division has multiple time recording systems across a number of sites, and different planning and resourcing infrastructures. These processes are linked via a series of fragmented spreadsheets and in-house legacy applications all covering core aspects of the business including business plans, operational deployment, and forecasts as well as project recharging and resource utilisation. This patchwork of systems prevents the executive decision making stream from rolling up project information into one single view in order to gain top-down visibility of the overall status of the project portfolio.

The wider impact of this infrastructure results in the following problems:

- *No strategic alignment*: For IT the question is how IT spending supports the corporate strategy. IT is faced with an overspend and missed deadlines because they lack visibility of their strategy, plans, performance, and costs. IT accountability and visibility are seen as the main deliverables in order to accelerate decision making based upon factual, tangible data. For IT the primary business challenge is to be able to create and demonstrate its value to the overall organisation. This is to be achieved by implementing a PPM process that would enable them not only to manage the day-to-day operations of their projects and resources but also to develop an holistic view of progress and performance. The goal is to develop a real-time link between strategic goals and operations.
- *Poor operational synergy*: At the operational level the IT resource management process is performed manually by using Excel spreadsheets. IT is unable to maintain these spreadsheets at a detailed level and additional tools are required to track staff time, which are not integrated with the planning infrastructure. These disparate data points and their inaccuracy result in a lack of ability to predict, manage and report on resource availability, project costs and staff effort. Not having accurate staff allocation information makes new work difficult to plan, and it is virtually impossible to report (in real time) on the progress and performance of key projects.
- *Fragmented technical infrastructure*: These multiple systems have created a technical jungle. A single standard just does not exist and this lack of technical synergy prevents the organisation from working in a consistent environment. As in scenario 1, this impacts on the ability of executive decision makers to source real-time information, forcing decisions to be based on estimations, or at worst, guesswork.
- *Poor reporting capability:* Another problem is communicating project performance goals downstream through layers of management. While top management are aware of strategic goals, most staff down the hierarchy do not fully understand their obligation to support these goals. In effect, IT is collecting, defining and displaying information based on different interpretations of the strategy. Because this information is incomplete or linked to particular functions, there is no means of centralising a coherent and meaningful system that management can

trust. The challenge for IT is to develop management information that pushes down and pulls up project performance metrics.

- *Excessive administration*: The spreadsheet based system makes day-to-day management of the process excessively manual and paper based. At one level this results in poor data quality and lack of revision control, often leading to the duplication and overwriting of key files. The excessive transfers of paper further impact on the system, sometimes causing crucial slippage on key projects, resulting in lost opportunities to recharge clients.

12.2.2   The business solution

The successful implementation of the PPM process for IT hinges on the ability to provide visibility of the strategic alignment of projects and resources, which can enable executives to ensure that IT is focusing on what matters to the overall business. The implementation gives executive and IT management a real-time view of which projects are being implemented in the organisation and an accurate reflection of their status in terms of staff utilisation and cost. This allows executive decision makers to understand how IT investments are being spent, how to eliminate duplicated efforts, how to identify which projects can be removed and which projects need to be recharged back to internal clients. An essential element is to ensure real-time detection for quicker resolution of project conflict.

12.2.3   The business benefits

PPM implementation helps IT achieve visibility by providing a means to ensure:

- *Improved resource utilisation*: Implementation allows IT to integrate all aspects of the resource and project management processes into one PPM process framework accessible via a dedicated PPM web based software solution. Executives, portfolio and resource managers are now able to see that their most valuable resources are working on the most strategic projects and are also now able to optimise the use of resources, enabling IT to accomplish more with less.
- *Improved planning and recharging*: IT is now able to plan and manage projects more efficiently. The implementation of standardised PPM has radically improved project cost accuracy, enabling timely recharging and billing to internal customers. The result has been a dramatic

increase in the number of billable hours realised and improvements in cash flow. IT is now able to reconcile, in real time, its contribution to the bottom line.

- *IT accountability*: Executives now know exactly how their project portfolio is progressing, and by adopting a practice of immediate and constant review of project performance, team members are now able to understand how the efforts of the IT team will be used to make critical decisions. Improved accuracy, visibility and transparency within the operational infrastructure of IT have enabled it to align its work with corporate goals. IT now has visibility and understanding of its contribution to the overall business. This increase in collaboration ensures that IT governance controls are being executed vis-à-vis the company strategy.

- *Real-time management reporting*: Real-time web based reporting technology has helped IT to reduce administrative time spent on management reporting. Instead of producing inaccurate monthly reports, managers are now able to report in real time on project performance and to deal with any roadblocks that may be impeding the success of a project.

- *Improved information flow and management*: The PPM process has streamlined many of IT's labour-intensive administration procedures. PPM document management capability has dramatically cut paperwork, improved data sharing, reconciliation and quality of data for management reports, and reduced conflict.

- *Executive visibility*: The biggest challenge facing executives was establishing IT as an influential partner in the business and determining the impact of IT initiatives on the bottom line. At the same time, they faced increasing pressure to meet newly established IT governance requirements and demands to improve IT's strategic alignment with corporate goals. To succeed under these competing mandates, executives had to gain confidence in IT's control over spending and activity. PPM implementation now enables executives to:
  - make and enforce rules for approval of spending;
  - ensure that IT spending is confined to approved work;
  - demonstrate IT's effectiveness to the business via personalised online reporting;
  - tie IT spending to strategy and focus on reducing costs while delivering greater value
  - make certain that IT is focused on the most strategic projects for the business
  - demonstrate IT's value by improving collaboration and communication between strategy and operations

- support the overall corporate strategy by driving the right balance of spending on business goals

- *Management visibility*: For IT managers the challenge was ensuring on-time, on-budget project delivery, while communicating real-time status to key portfolio stakeholders and the executive decision making stream. It was essential for IT managers to be able to marry their operational activities with an understanding of corporate strategy and to see how their key projects supported the implementation of the business's core goals. It was also essential for executives to see how IT managers could tie their spending to strategy and focus on reducing costs while delivering greater value. IT managers are now able to reconcile spend with strategy and demonstrate a tangible alignment with the business units it serves. PPM implementation has now enabled IT managers to:
  - assist corporate executives and business unit leaders in understanding the role of IT in the business strategy
  - access a comprehensive view of demand, plans to execute demand, project performance, and costs associated with projects
  - support corporate strategy by driving the right spending priorities
  - make decisions based on tangible, factual, real-time data
  - partner with the business to correctly set and communicate priorities
  - increase communication and collaboration with customers – with real-time status
  - access personalised reporting views and shared performance dashboards
  - reduce overspending through the capture, assessment, assignment and monitoring of risks and issues on all work
  - achieve increased visibility of project status to facilitate decision making and control expectations

- *Team visibility*: For IT it was clear that team members had the difficult job of trying to juggle multiple demands on their time while collaborating with others. It was essential for team members to be able to communicate effectively and ensure that their activities were understood by their managers and the organisation at large. PPM implementation has enabled team members to:
  - ensure collaboration between IT project teams
  - improve communication between IT and other business units
  - give team members control over project documents and schedules
  - provide teams with the ability to understand and prioritise their work in the context of real-time business plans, and provide real-time project status to managers and beneficiaries

12.3   Scenario 3: improving service delivery through strategic project alignment

12.3.1   The business challenges

Your primary objective is to use the PPM process to improve service delivery throughout the organisation, by improving internal project and resource management as the best means of providing visibility of organisational activities.

The challenge is to build an infrastructure that moves the organisation from a department based resource and project management process into a strategically driven framework directed by the PPMT. In addition, this system needs to enforce greater project accountability by developing a real-time strategic alignment between the performance of key projects and their impact on corporate goals.

There is no alignment with operational processes such as project planning, forecasting and resourcing. The result is an inability of the organisation to improve service delivery and maximise its capacity to process new business opportunities. The consequence is a misalignment between the project and resource management processes, having a knock-on impact on the operational capability of company divisions.

Other inherent issues include:

- *Fragmented business applications*: At the lowest level, business processes are supported by a series of manual resource management and project planning systems. These are operated through a collection of project-centric plans scattered across the business infrastructure. The result is a disjointed system that lacks visibility of how the business can manage resources and projects in real time. This fragmented network of applications prohibits executives and managers from spotting key operational redundancies, preventing them from reducing risk exposure.
- *Semi-autonomous business processes*: A major roadblock to improving overall service performance stems from the fact that many of the organisation's departments and teams are acting independently of each other. For example, each department has its own resource allocation systems that are not integrated into project plans or time recording capabilities. These disparate data points and their inaccuracy result in a lack of ability to predict, manage and report on resource availability, project costs and staff effort. The results cascade up the business as projects slip and budgets are not being met, hitting the bottom line. In addition, each department is collecting, defining and displaying information

based on a different interpretation of the strategy. Because this information is incomplete or linked to particular functions, there is no means
of centralising a coherent and meaningful system that management can
trust.

- *Latency within the decision making process*: Diffuse operational
  processes cause latency within the executive decision making stream.
  For example, managers are hindered by their inability to extract
  accurate, relevant real-time information about resource availability,
  project costs, risks and milestone deliverables. They are therefore
  unable to keep senior executives informed with a single end-to-end
  report. Executives are unable to obtain the right information at the
  right time to effectively understand the present position of the business in order to ward off unwelcome surprises and jump on potential
  opportunities before the competition.

12.3.2 The business solution

A major reason for the business to implement a PPM process is to create
a real-time link between the strategy of the business and the quality of its
project delivery execution process, to ensure better service delivery. This
includes resource allocation and project milestone management and how
they are impacting projects being delivered to customers. It is imperative
that the PPM process provide a single point of entry, keeping all the
processes consistent, current and complete. It also essential that staff work
within only one solution, eliminating the time it takes to move between
applications.

12.3.3 The business benefits

PPM implementation delivers a better understanding of the business –
fusing together the strategic and operational processes to maximise
service efficiency, bringing such benefits as:

- *Strategic and operational alignment*: PPM has given executives the
  ability to tie strategic and operational requirements closer together into
  a single end-to-end view. They now have a consistent and complete
  view of the business's work stack. The result is a process that gives
  controlled and predictable execution of strategic planning.
- *Real-time business visibility*: PPM has enabled executives to gain a
  clear view of performance and its impact on the business. The business

has now gained a higher level of predictability and visibility in the accuracy of its performance measurements and their impact on the bottom line.

- *Real-time corporate accountability*: Ensuring that operational staff are accountable to the business strategy is a major benefit. The complexity of traditional task based planning did not give management the ability to accurately identify resource waste, slipping projects and overspend. For example, executives now have real-time information on the status of the critical project milestones and resource availability that drive the business. They are now able to identify whether key projects will be completed on time, why deadlines have been moved, who moved them and what the cost will be.

- *Operational synergy and flexibility*: PPM implementation has provided the business with enormous operational flexibility. For example, milestone tracking and scenario modelling have enabled the business to respond quickly to customer needs by allowing it to determine in real time which projects need assistance, which projects are running smoothly and which projects need to be changed. Operational synergy has been achieved by linking this to more accurate and easier-to-use resource capabilities within one single interface. The PPM process now provides instant visibility of resource allocation throughout the entire global resource pool, making it quick and easy to locate and deploy appropriately skilled staff. Skills shortfalls and training requirements can be easily identified and addressed, ensuring a clear focus on the demand and supply dynamic. The overall effect is an improvement of the business's budgeting and planning capabilities, which has given an essential insight into the organisation and flexibility needed to react quickly to changing market conditions.

- *Centralised risk management*: PPM implementation has provided a consistent approach to risk management. The business has gained the benefits of an easily controlled and web publishable risk register that helps it to focus on active risk management, delivering control over key project initiatives.

- *Project accountability*: Executives now know exactly how their project portfolio is progressing, and by adopting a practice of immediate and constant review, team members are now able to understand how the efforts of the team will be used to make critical decisions. Improved accuracy, visibility and transparency within the infrastructure across the company have enabled them to align their work with corporate goals.

- *Real-time management reporting*: With PPM web based reporting facilities, the business is able to reconcile flexible and powerful data from multiple departments and data sources. This one single real-time view provides a centralised, coherent and meaningful system that management can trust. PPM implementation has given executives real-time reporting of slipping projects and budget allocations, as well as enabling managers to plan and report multiple scenarios in terms of time, costs and skills and how they impact the bottom line. PPM has enabled the business's operational process to engage with its strategic vision in real time.

12.4   Scenario 4: Preparing the groundwork for PPM by implementing a standardised project and resource management software solution

12.4.1   The business challenges

Your primary objective is to help prepare the business for PPM by implementing a single, integrated software solution to best practice project and resource management throughout the enterprise.

What problems do you face? The enterprise has a series of fragmented time recording, planning and resource infrastructures covering business plans and operational deployment issues as well as project and resource demands. The result is a disjointed system that lacks visibility of how you can manage resources and projects within the business. Your main problems are:

- inefficiencies in the actual tracking of time against specific project tasks
- inability to plan accurately within a multi-project environment
- lack of revision control over resource allocation spreadsheets and MS Project plans
- double booking, poor skills utilisation and conflict over allocation of key resources
- poorly recorded data, preventing executives from analysing true project performance
- disparate and differentiated resource and project information pools
- poor coordination between individual project managers and project teams, impacting on divisions' ability to quickly absorb new revenue generating business opportunities
- inability to forecast and accurately plan new projects and assign resources
- skills shortages and misutilisation of resources

- unreliable and inefficient methods of securing people via networking and bartering practices
- lack of automated resource support tools
- lack of quality control over project time related information released to the business

In order to achieve a significant improvement in your business effectiveness you need to replace your inaccurate and unmanageable project and resource management capability with a more flexible, integrated solution.

12.4.2 The business solution

The solution is to implement a system that allows the business to control resource and project management processes from one single, integrated tool-set.

You choose to roll out enterprise timesheet and expense tracking, together with a planning and resourcing management system, to ensure that the business benefits from an integrated, web based solution.

The solution linkage allows staff to log actual time expended against individual project tasks, providing accurate and detailed information. This allows the business to plan, manage and report fully on the resources, costs, effort and duration associated with projects. By providing a clear view of resource utilisation, the solution enables the business to plan projects quicker and more efficiently, while enabling the accurate collection of project data to provide a solid foundation for building a productivity database.

12.4.3 The business benefits

Implementing a single integrated timesheet, expense, planning and resource management solution has brought tangible benefits. For example, the business is now able to:

- track time expended against project tasks and deliver accurate data on actual use of staff time
- plan with virtual resources without disturbing current project schedules
- search via a centralised skills matrix to allow for the suitable and timely allocation of staff when planning projects
- overcome project conflicts by integrating multi-project interaction within a single resource and planning pool

- plan dependency risks by allowing project managers to view possible roadblocks to project success
- use a centralised source that links actions with projects and owners for timely and traceable actions
- perform more effective benchmarking of internal services against external service provision
- adopt an automated and centralised method of tracking and monitoring work
- carry out product based planning across all projects, with delivery of more accurate project management, scheduling and planning
- adopt a quick and easily unified method of identifying underutilised staff and/or those with obsolete skills, who could be cross-trained and used to support overworked staff or replace contractors
- track relationships between delivery and spend more closely with 'earned value analysis'
- have available more effective management information to make quicker, more informed decisions
- improve utilisation through better load spread with the use of real-time and online decision support material, allowing fast searching for suitable staff when planning work
- have available accurate data on actual use of staff time
- identify duplication of effort (for example, in people management, invoicing and so on)

CHAPTER 13

PPM action checklists

These checklists are designed to complement the PPM processes explained within the book by providing you with key features (section 13.1) and questions (section 13.2) concerning how to help implement and maintain a successful PPM process.

13.1 Checklist of key features

The checklist below provides a full list of key features within a PPM solution. This breakdown covers strategic PPM capability as well as the solution's operational project delivery and management features including timesheet, expenses management, task based project planning, resource management, risk management, contractor management and business information tracking.

13.1.1 Portfolio management features

- ideas management
- portfolio selection and prioritisation
- out-of-the-box scoring
- scenario modelling
- 'what if' modelling
- capability planning
- trend reports
- business warning indicators
- current position based forecasting

13.1.2 Programme management features

- business performance monitoring
- top-down business tracking
- opportunity closing

- business planning
- governance planning

13.1.3   Timesheet and expense management features

- timesheet tracking
- timesheet approval
- project billing
- expense management forecast vs actuals

13.1.4   Resource management features

- resource alignment and levelling
- resource scheduling
- supply and demand processing

13.1.5   Project management features

- MS Project integration
- milestone tracking
- project modelling
- best practice
- project control

13.1.6   Budgeting and financial management features

- budget forecasting
- budget tracking
- expense tracking
- financial modelling
- operating costs
- margin tracking
- invoice tracking

13.1.7   Risk management features

- risk register
- mitigation management

- action review
- risk heat maps

13.1.8 Contract management features

- contract management
- contract review

13.1.9 Business dashboard features

- direct entry views
- drill-down capability

13.1.10 Role based features

- executive dashboard
- portfolio dashboard
- programme dashboard
- project management dashboard
- resource management dashboard
- delivery management dashboard
- supply and demand dashboard

13.1.11 Business reporting features

- context reports
- custom reports
- out-of-the-box business intelligence

13.1.12 Communication management features

- data distribution
- knowledge and document handling

13.1.13 Process support and workflow management features

- process support dashboards
- contact management

- stakeholder management
- issues and benefits analysis
- project request and issue tracking
- partner relationship management
- helpdesk support

13.1.14 Integration management features

- enterprise applications
- accounting applications
- MS Project integration

13.2 Checklist of key questions

This checklist of questions can used when building a PPM framework. It is particularly useful when performing a health check and implementing the initial PPM model as part of a PoB deployment.

13.2.1 Alignment of business strategy and project goals

- Does the project team have pertinent knowledge of overall corporate goals?
- Are project parameters defined in terms of the parameters of the overall portfolio?
- Do team structures represent a probable approach to reaching project and corporate goals?
- Do team members understand their role in contributing to overall organisational goals?

13.2.2 Portfolio mix

- What strategy is utilised in determining the right mix of projects in the portfolio?

13.2.3 Project prioritisation and selection processes

- Can you describe the formal and informal mechanisms used to evaluate the priority of projects in the stream?

- On what criteria is project selection based?
- What role does executive management play in the project selection process?

13.2.4 Project initiation and approval processes

- What are the formal and informal project initiation processes used in the business?
- What mechanisms are used to identify projects as approved?
- What mechanisms are used to tell management when approved projects in the stream can begin?
- What mechanisms exist to tell management the effect newly initiated projects have on other projects in the portfolio?

13.2.5 Roles and responsibilities

- Are project managers' roles and responsibilities defined in terms of overall portfolio goals?
- What activities currently comprise the work of project managers? And of project sponsors?
- Who plans projects (work breakdown structure, dependencies)?

13.2.6 The framework

- Do programme rules and procedures consider impacts across the overall portfolio?
- Does an infrastructure exist to support cross-programme communication and collaboration?
- Are overall portfolio goals considered in conflict resolution processes?
- What tools, processes or methodologies are used for project planning and tracking?
- What tools, processes or methodologies are used for resource planning?

13.2.7 Estimation processes

- How do project teams estimate project size?
- How do project teams estimate task duration?
- Is estimation effective/accurate?

13.2.8 Resource pool and availability

- How do project teams identify resource needs?
- How is the resource pool designated?
- How are resource conflicts negotiated and resolved?
- What skills inventory process exists?
- Does resource acquisition strategy match the resource requirements reflected in the approved mix of projects in the portfolio?
- Do project teams have the resources required to accomplish projects in the portfolio?

13.2.9 Project status

- What mechanism exists to determine the status of all projects in the portfolio?
- Do any projects not comply with status reporting requirements?
- How accurate are project schedule and resource utilisation predictions?
- What factors create schedule and planned resource deviations?

13.2.10 'Go/kill/hold/fix' decisions

- Is there a process for cancelling projects?
- Are 'go/kill/hold/fix' decisions made at portfolio level?
- What criteria are used for these decisions?
- At what points in the project life cycle are these decisions made?

13.2.11 Key project and organisational interfaces

- What mechanisms exist to determine the impact of schedule changes on other projects in the portfolio and their related priorities?
- What other organisational processes exist with which a project portfolio solution may need to interface?

Below is a list of the material that we consulted for the book, and which we also recommend as further reading.

Aitken, I. (2003) *Value-driven IT Management. Computer Weekly* Professional Series. Oxford: Butterworth Heinemann.

Berkshire Consultancy and Atlantic Global (2006) Project Portfolio Management Round Table.

CFO Research Services in collaboration with Propix Software (2004) *Budgeting and Planning at Midsize Companies: When Spreadsheets Alone Are Not Enough.*

Ciliberti, R. (2005) *Using Project Portfolio Management to Improve Business Value.* White Paper by IBM.

Collins, K. (2005) *Eight Reasons to Consider Hosted or On-Demand MRM Applications Analysis.* Report by Gartner Research.

Cooper, R. and Edgett, S. (2000) *New Problems, New Solutions: Making Portfolio Management More Effective.* Working Paper 9, Stage Gate Inc.

Cooper, R. and Edgett, S. (2001) *Portfolio Management for New Products: Picking the Winners.* Working Paper 11, Stage Gate Inc.

Cooper, R. and Edgett, S. (2006) *10 Ways to Make Better Portfolio and Project Selection Decisions.* Feature article by Stage Gate Inc.

Cooper, R. and Edgett, S. (2006) *Portfolio Management: Fundamental for New Product Success.* Working Paper 12, Stage Gate Inc.

Evolution of the PMO: Agile Portfolio Management (2004) White Paper by Grant Thornton.

Gartner Research (2002) *It's Time for the Real-time Enterprise: Extracting Real Value from Your Business.* Special report.

Gartner Research (2003) *Business Process Fusion: Enabling the Real-time Enterprise.* Special report.

Kaplan, J. D. (2005) *Strategic IT Portfolio Management: Governing Enterprise Transformation.* Report by Pittiglio Rabin Todd and McGrath Inc.

KPMG (2005) *Global Programme Management Survey – A UK Perspective.*

Levine, H. (2005) *Components of a Project Portfolio Management Process (Part One – Selecting Projects for the Pipeline).* Report for Sciforma Corporation.

Levine, H. (2005) *Components of a Project Portfolio Management Process (Part Two – Managing the Pipeline)*. Report for Sciforma Corporation.

Levine, H. (2005) *Components of a Project Portfolio Management Process (Part Three – Executing Project Portfolio Management)*. Report for Sciforma Corporation.

Levine, H. (2005) *Project Portfolio Management (A Song without Words?)*. Report for Sciforma Corporation.

Light, M., Hotle, M., Stang, D. and Heine, J. (2005) *Project Management Office: The IT Control Tower*. Report by Gartner Research.

Light, M., Rosser, B. and Hayward, S. (2005) *Realizing the Benefits of Project Portfolio Management*. Report by Gartner Research.

Maizlish, B. and Handler, R. (2005) *IT Portfolio Management Step-By-Step: Unlocking the Business Value of Technology*. Hoboken: John Wiley.

McFarlan, F. W. (1981) 'Portfolio approach to information systems'. *Harvard Business Review* (September–October): 142–50.

Major, P. (2005) *Turning Strategy into Action: The Real Value of Enterprise Project Management*. White Paper by Management Framework Ltd.

Merkhofer, L. (2004) *Choosing the Wrong Portfolio of Projects: And What Your Organisation Can Do About It*. Report for Max Wideman's Project Management Wisdom.

Pring, B. (2005) *Cost, Focus and Speed Drive Continued Adoption of Application Service Provider*. Report by Gartner Research.

Stang, D. (2004) *PPM Challenges and Process Inefficiencies*. Report by Gartner Research.

Stang, D. (2006) *When Evaluating PPM Vendors, Include SAAS and On-Demand Options*. Report by Gartner Research.